CW00517105

The
Bridgewater Canal

Ron & Marlene Freethy

AURORA
PUBLISHING

© Ron and Marlene Freethy

This edition published by:
Aurora Enterprises Ltd
Unit 9, Bradley Fold Trading Estate,
Radcliffe Moor Road, Bradley Fold,
Bolton BL2 6RT.
Tel: 01204 370752

ISBN 1 85926 070 5

Front cover photograph:
The Bridgewater Canal at Lymm.

Back cover photograph:
Anglers on the banks of the canal at
Castlefield prove that the water is clean.

Title page photograph:
The Castlefield Complex.

Designed, printed and bound by
MFP Design & Print,
Longford Trading Estate,
Thomas Street,
Stretford,
Manchester M32 0JT.
Tel: 0161 864 4540

*The Castlefield complex is now one of Manchester's most
attractive areas of the city.*

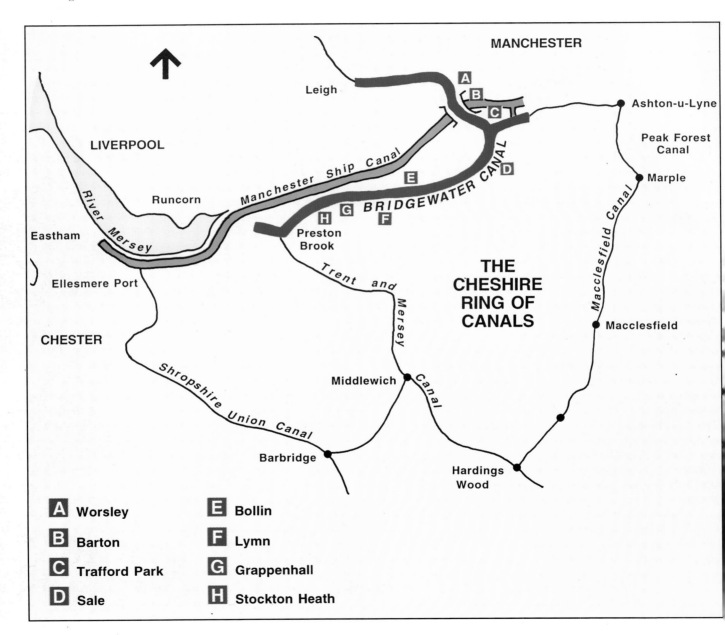

MANCHESTER

Leigh

LIVERPOOL

Ashton-u-Lyne

Peak Forest
Canal

Marple

Runcorn

Manchester Ship Canal

BRIDGEWATER CANAL

Macclesfield Canal

Eastham

River Mersey

Ellesmere Port

Preston
Brook

Trent and Mersey Canal

THE
CHESHIRE
RING OF
CANALS

Macclesfield

CHESTER

Shropshire Union Canal

Middlewich

Barbridge

Hardings
Wood

A Worsley

B Barton

C Trafford Park

D Sale

E Bollin

F Lymn

G Grappenhall

H Stockton Heath

*Above: Canal-side
cottages at Lymm.*

*Top right: Barge scene
at canal bank.*

*Bottom right:
Worsley Hall.*

Left: Preston Brook Marina.

Opposite page: View of the Bridgewater Canal looking back from Waterloo Bridge.

Left: The Packet House is not Tudor in origin, but was constructed on the banks of the Bridgewater Canal.

Right: The dock area at Worsley is the oldest still working in any canal in Britain.

Contents

Introduction
& Acknowledgments

WE HAD OFTEN thought of preparing a book on the Bridgewater Canal following a volume we had published on the River Mersey. What intrigued us was to discover how the canal systems of North Western England linked in to the existing river systems, especially the Irwell, the Mersey and the Weaver.

Of all the canals, the Bridgewater was the most interesting because it was the first and the engineering problems had to be solved from first principles.

The chance to work on the Bridgewater Canal came as a result of a meeting with Evelyn Draper of BBC Greater Manchester Radio and later of BBC Radio Merseyside who commissioned documentaries on North Western Watercourses including the Bridgewater. John Clayton of BBC Radio Lancashire also contributed humerous anecdotes and practical assistance.

In the course of researching and recording these programmes during 1995 several people were of great assistance and were equally enthusiastic about the book. We have listed those who helped us, not in alphabetical order but in the sequence where we located them as we journeyed along the canal from Leigh to its one time link to the Mersey.

The wardens at Pennington Flash on the outskirts of Leigh are proud of the wildlife and especially the birds recorded in and around what was once an industrial landscape and gave up their time to walk all the footpaths with us and incorporated an informative stroll along the canal bank. We had a wonderful day sheltering in a bird hide away from the swirling snow, watching a colourful jay and having just missed seeing the third kingfisher of the day.

At Worsley Boat Yard we sat drinking coffee with co-proprietor Marylin Frear in her house overlooking the boats and listening to an enthusiast working on his boat in England's oldest canal dry dock.

The staff at the Information Centres around the Castlefield Basin in Central Manchester were helpful and cheerful and interpreted the maze of waterways which link the Irwell, the Rochdale Canal and of course the Bridgewater. They all remarked with a smile that the Duke's Cut was the first to bring prosperity to the city.

Our journey through the industrial complexities of Trafford Park and the Barton Aqueduct brought genuine interest rather than either amusement or complaint at our intrusion. The workers we found still had a love for the Bridgewater Canal and most knew that it was initially responsible for the Park producing so many jobs.

Janet Edwards, the National Trust's Information Officer at Dunham Massey, was a mine of information and allowed us to make use of a number of photographs as well as allowing us full rein to use our own cameras.

The Vicar of Daresbury church proved to be a devotee of Lewis Carroll and this helped greatly to develop our own enthusiasm for the project. The staff of Norton Priory were equally enthusiastic and the ruins and gardens provide a perfect backdrop to the canal. Our thanks are due to Margaret Warhurst the curator and her staff.

Boating people are always friendly and inquisitive and those enjoying cruising around Worsley, Lymm, Preston Brook and Runcorn provided lots of encouragement to us carrying recording equipment, making notes and taking photographs. "Tha needs an 'imalayan sherpa to do this job", said one old boater "buy the sel' a boat and do't job reight."

All those mentioned above helped us to discover the Bridgewater in particular, but we also had two other sources concerned with the canals of North Western England in general. The Manchester Ship Canal Company were encouraging and allowed us to use their archives. The Port Director Jim Chilton and the Chairman and Managing Director Robert Hough were both a mine of information.

The staff of the Boat Museum at Ellesmere Port provided a link which we could have forged nowhere else. Here we could see boats which had actually worked on the Bridgewater. Our special thanks go to Tony Hurst the Director, to Doyle Rush the archivist and to the Public Relations' Officer Carole Winstanley who showed commendable patience in taking us round the site on several occasions. At the end of our journey along the Bridgewater Canal we therefore felt it essential to include a postscript dealing with the Boat Museum which has so much relevance to the work of the Duke's Cut.

There have been many academic books dealing with the Bridgewater Canal. This is not intended to be another. Neither is it intended to be a book of large photographs with long captions. What then are our aims? It is a record of our personal journey along a wonderful old waterway and during which we hope to help our readers to plan quiet walks through the history, natural history and industrial archaeology of the canal. This book is now complete but we will not stop walking the Old Duke's Cut because we know that there is still much more to discover, many more old photographs to find and many new friends to meet.

Ron & Marlene Freethy

CHAPTER ONE

In the Beginning...

A LOOK AT a modern map gives the impression that the Bridgewater Canal follows a complicated course from its junction with the Leeds to Liverpool Canal near Leigh to Runcorn. Its twisting journey seems to pass through one of the most industrialised landscapes in Europe.

If, however, one examines the origins of Britain's first true canal, the reverse is seen to be the case. It was actually the canal which spawned the industry. Initially, it was constructed to carry coal to the then small town of Manchester from the mines at Worsley which then expanded dramatically once a market was opened up. The canal immediately reduced the price of coal, as a barge pulled over water could deliver huge volumes of coal in comparison with the strings of packhorses moving ponderously across the rough moorland tracks.

The Industrial Revolution evolved because of the bringing together of coal and water. It was the Bridgewater Canal which was directly responsible for the growth of Manchester, for the swift spread of industry into the heart of the Cheshire countryside and which eventually swamped such rural estates as Trafford Park.

As industry grew the Bridgewater was extended and side shoots were cut to link new industries to the canal; businessmen are never slow to take advantage of innovations once they have proved themselves capable of generating profits and increasing numbers of canals were built. Most were linked, however tenuously they may seem these days, to the Bridgewater. The evolution of this waterway system accounts for the fact that the Bridgewater Canal has a shape somewhat resembling a crescent, which once linked with the Mersey estuary at one end and the Leeds to Liverpool Canal at the other.

The length of the main line was eventually 37.6 kilometres (23 miles and 3 furlongs) but there were a number of branches which added a further 26.4 kilometres (16 miles and 3 furlongs). There are still 101 bridges, although these are not numbered sequentially. Number one, for example, links into the Trent and Mersey and number 101 is situated close to the link with the Rochdale canal in the heart of Manchester.

The Bridgewater is an example of a contour canal which sticks to a line 25.2 metres (83 feet) above sea level and thus the need for expensive locks was alleviated. The art, or should it be the science, of lock construction took time to evolve and the Bridgewater, which was the prototype for all the others, had to await later developments which its presence actually stimulated. The Hulme Locks later linked the Bridgewater with the Manchester Ship Canal and another dramatic set of locks connected first with the Mersey estuary and later to the Ship Canal. These have sadly been removed at a point close to the Waterloo Bridge, but there are ambitious plans in hand to restore this once vital link.

The eastern section of the Bridgewater Canal now (but not originally) runs through a largely industrialised area, but the western section has retained much of its rural character and is particularly and increasingly popular with pleasure craft.

The Bridgewater is now an important link in what has become known as the Cheshire Ring. A footpath follows much of this ring and this is by far the best way to explore the canal. Boating is the most pleasurable method of discovery but it is not always very convenient to stop and moor up

The Bridgewater Barge Horses on Parade, 1930.

at each and every point of interest.

In order to follow the present line of the canal it is best to begin at Leigh, where some will argue that you are actually on the Leeds to Liverpool Canal. We prefer to say that the two canals share the link and therefore the Bridgewater should be considered to start near the halfway point — which is round about Leigh. We will therefore start our journey at Pennington Flash Country Park at Leigh and then move on towards Worsley where the Canal Age in England began.

From Worsley the canal is followed to the famous Barton Aqueduct which now crosses the Manchester Ship Canal and thence through the complex of Trafford Park and onwards to the important Water Meetings at Stretford. From here. a vital branch cuts into the centre of Manchester whilst the main line continues onwards through Sale and Lymm to the junction with the Trent and Mersey at Preston Brook. The final lap then takes us along another major branch from the main line, this one leading to Runcorn, the Manchester Ship Canal and the mighty Mersey estuary.

Before describing the journey along the Bridgewater Canal something should be said of the men who financed, organised and planned the construction of the first English canal and which set the pattern for the mania which drove ambitious businessmen wild between 1760 and 1820. It was only the coming of the equally frantic railway mania which brought canal speculation to an end. Did the railways ruin those who made money speculating on canals? The wise certainly did not suffer — they merely bought shares in the railway. Later, the same men purchased or retained a controlling interest in the canals in order to have the power to absorb all opposition.

The Duke of Bridgewater initiated the Canal Age and even as his waterway was opened between Worsley and Barton he was wise enough to predict that the only threat to the new system was likely to be the railways. All transport historians mention the Duke's foresight but as we will prove later, this wise man also experimented with steam propulsion.

Francis Egerton, the Third Duke of Bridgewater, had money and a single minded drive but he had something else which was probably even more vital — he was a fine judge of men and once he selected a man for a job, he invariably allowed him to get on with it.

The Canal Age had, however, not just one father but three; Francis Egerton (1736-1803), his engineer James Brindley (1716-1772) and the most underated of the three, the indefatigable John Gilbert (1724-1795). The lives of these three giants of the Industrial Revolution will be considered in the next chapter.

CHAPTER TWO

Three Canal Kings

THE FACT THAT Francis Egerton ever became the 3rd Duke of Bridgewater was the result of not one but several family tragedies. His father produced three children by his first marriage — a daughter and two sons who both died young. His second marriage brought him eight children including four sons. Francis, born in 1736, was the youngest of these four boys and the only one to survive to maturity. When his father died, Francis was only eight and within a year his mother, who was then in her early 50s, married a man some 25 years her junior.

Although he obviously survived, Francis was never a healthy child and suffered from tuberculosis; despite this his new stepfather lost no time in packing him off to boarding school. Perhaps he did not wish his new wife to spend too much time and energy on an ailing child.

It is therefore not surprising to find that in later life Francis Egerton found relationships with the opposite sex rather difficult to sustain. By the time he was eleven this insecure child had been named as the Third Duke of Bridgewater and, therefore, needed to be "properly educated", but Eton did not prove to be a happy period in his life.

Like many young men of wealth, Francis eventually set out on the Grand Tour of Europe and it was during his travels with his tutor, the learned Robert Wood, that he became fascinated by canals. We know how impressive the Grand Languedoc Canal still is which runs from the Mediterranean to the Bay of Biscay. Coming from a country criss-crossed by rough roads along which rattled bone shaking carriages, the smooth passage of barges along these gentle and predictable watercourses of the continent must have seemed like a miracle to young Francis.

The young and very eligible (at least from a financial point of view) Duke of Bridgewater, on returning from his trip, turned his attentions and his fortunes to the pursuit of a wife, and also to the risks of the gaming table. Neither brought him any joy. Francis became engaged to Jane Revell but she may well have found him boring, financially reckless, unhealthy and perhaps, if his later life is anything to go by, unkempt in appearance. Jane eventually switched her affections to George Warren a young, personable and energetic squire from Cheshire who was almost as rich as Francis. He may well have shown signs of not being willing to risk his fortune on the gaming-tables. Such a man would have been a much better matrimonial prospect.

It was not a case of once bitten twice shy and the young Duke then courted the beautiful widow, Elizabeth the Duchess of Hamilton. He also failed to sustain this relationship, the engagement being broken off by Elizabeth who eventually married the Duke of Argyll.

Forever after, the Duke of Bridgewater turned his back on women and also on the gaming-tables and the racecourse at Newmarket. He made the construction of a canal the eventual key to his fortunes and the one lasting love of his life. Some may point out that risking his fortune on the construction of a canal was the biggest gamble of his life. He returned to his home base at Worsley more and more regularly and along with James Brindley and John Gilbert he dragged the North West of England into the forefront of the Industrial Revolution.

He became an eccentric, never clean or tidy, but shambled about the workings of his mines and canal talking to few people and then only when absolutely necessary. He otherwise lived the austere life of a recluse. He hated writing letters and visitors to Worsley Hall were not welcome. He is alleged to have made the point that if he visited a house, he could leave whenever he wanted, whilst those who came to him could, and far too often did, outstay their welcome.

Francis did not forget everything that his tutor Robert Wood, had taught him and as his finances began to improve, when his canal at last yielded profits, he built up an impressive collection of works of art. Many thought that he lacked personality, but there is no doubt that the Duke of Bridgewater was intelligent and not without the occasional flash of humour. He worked himself very hard around his coalmines at Worsley and also along his canal as it was cut towards Manchester. He expected all those he employed to do the same. He was apt to shamble out of the shadows and confront slackers. One group of workers returning late from their lunch break told the Duke that they had failed to hear the church bell strike one. The Duke accepted the excuse but reacted by fitting a new set of chimes to the clock and which then struck not one but thirteen!

He was also occasionally capable of accepting the humour of others. He approached another late comer who told him that he had been delayed by his wife who had just given birth to twins. "You must take what God gives", the Duke commented. "Aye My Lord, he gives me the bairns and gives all the brass to thee." Whilst this sounds like a piece of Lancashire's tongue-in-cheek folklore it does seem to have a grain of truth in it because the Duke gave his employee a guinea, which was a considerable sum in those days, and then shambled away laughing.

His workmen do seem to have had a genuine affection for the Duke of Bridgewater, almost certainly because he often appeared among them, even if he did not usually say anything. He also regularly travelled along his canal using one of his coaches which had been mounted on a barge.

In the later Railway Age many employers established what became known as a 'Tommy Shop'. This supplied the workmen and their families with essential groceries but often at inflated prices which was a subtle way of cheating the men to work for lower wages and keep the costs of their masters down. It was the Duke of Bridgewater who initiated this scheme, but he played fair with all. The families of his workers could run up bills at local shops and once a month the traders presented the accounts to the Duke's clerks who paid them and subtracted the money from the mens' wages. Everyone seemed satisfied with this arrangement which suggests that all participants in the scheme played fair.

There are also many instances of the Duke's consideration of the poor and there was a rule which applied around the coal wharves; those who could only afford a basket of fuel were to be served before those who arrived with a horse and cart.

Francis Egerton proved in his early life to be a very poor judge of women but he could certainly make sound judgements with regard to the men he placed in important positions in his business enterprises. He employed many able engineers and administrators but two stand out above all others. These were James Brindley and John Gilbert.

James Brindley was born of farming stock in 1716 at Tunstead which is just a short distance from Buxton. He followed the family line, as most lads of the period were obliged to do, but as he laboured on the farm fields his mind was always focused on the methods of constructing and maintaining water mills. The models which young Brindley made of water mills became locally famous. James must have been delighted when, at the age of 17, he was apprenticed to Abraham Bennet, a millwright from Macclesfield. He was later able to set up in business on his own account.

Through his life James Brindley never totally mastered the art of reading and writing but he proved to have a wonderful memory and an incisive and inventive brain. The educational system of modern

times would, we think, have diagnosed James Brindley as an intelligent scholar but one who may have been inflicted by severe dyslexia. In some ways Brindley's inability to read may have helped his development as an engineer. He could not read and therefore be tempted to copy the work of others and thus he developed new techniques based very much on first principles.

Because of the genius of his apprentice, Abraham Bennet became the most prosperous millwright in the Peak District and James Brindley's name and skills had reached the ears of Earl Gower who had extensive estates in the region. The Earl was the brother-in-law of Francis Egerton and when the lad became the Duke of Bridgewater, he was appointed as one of his guardians, the others being the Duke of Bedford and Samuel Egerton of Tatton Park. Earl Gower was himself interested in the development of canals, as he had a large investment in the pottery industry and realised the value of transporting such delicate items over smooth water in preference to bumping along over rough roads.

No doubt the Duke of Bridgewater discussed his canal project with his brother-in-law and had the good sense to overlook James Brindley's lack of literary skills and rough speech but to rely instead upon his natural genius. It was a wise choice as the Bridgewater Canal Act had its first reading on 23rd March 1759 and was open as far as Barton by 17 July 1761 cutting down the journey time from the mines to Manchester considerably. Then came the first major problem. How could the canal be dropped down to the Irwell to enable the river to carry the barges into the heart of Manchester?

James Brindley then rewarded the Duke for his

faith. He reasoned that it was far too expensive an exercise to lock the canal down to the Irwell which, like all rivers, was subject to lack of water in dry weather and a surfeit following rain or snow-melt. It would be far better, he reasoned, to ignore the Irwell altogether. Brindley suggested the construction of an aqueduct across the Irwell valley, but the very idea of such a enterprise was laughed at by his more literate and verbose critics. The Duke sensibly backed Brindley, the aqueduct worked, Manchester had a direct link independent of river fluctuations, the Duke's stretched finances improved at a stroke and Brindley's future as a canal builder of accepted genius was assured. Had Brindley not died in 1772 he would have continued hard at work for the Duke and other speculators and who knows what the two may have achieved. Brindley, like the Duke himself, had the ability to recognise the potential of others and Whitaker, his own personal steward, was an able and very reliable understudy. He supervised and even initiated many new techniques in the early years of canal construction.

In an amazingly short period Brindley's reputation was established and in 1769 the Cavendish family, anxious to have a transport system carrying coal, lead and iron to and from the Staveley area of Derbyshire, employed him. The Chesterfield Canal must have given James Brindley pleasure as it enabled him to return in triumph to work in his native county, and help to increase its prosperity.

So far we have fallen into the trap which has ensnared so many other writers working on the history of the Bridgewater Canal. There were not two but three men of genius employed during the construction of England's first canal. To describe John Gilbert (1724-1795) as merely the Duke's land agent is to do him a great injustice. He was a fine and imaginative engineer in his own right, but had one additional and quite vital ability — he was a financial administrator of great skill. The Bridgewater Canal only succeeded because of the combined abilities of the three and John Gilbert's contribution is far too often underrated. All three men had to solve problems, both financial and engineering, literally as they went along and needed courage as well as ability.

John Gilbert was Staffordshire born and at the age of only twelve he was apprenticed to the famous engineering company of Matthew Bolton. The experience gained under Bolton's direction was no doubt useful later as he helped solve the problems posed during the building of the first canal. When John was only 19 his father died and he had to leave the employ of Matthew Bolton and take over the management of the family lime works. Here he came into contact with the Earl of Gower and once again the Duke's brother-in-law was instrumental in fitting the human element of the jig saw of the Bridgewater Canal into place. Perhaps Gower was a more important catalyst in the construction of the canal than has ever been acknowledged.

Through the influence of the Earl of Gower, Gilbert was appointed to survey the Duke of Bridgewater's coal mines at Worsley and impressed the latter so much that by 1757 he was living along with his family in a wing of the Duke's home at Worsley Old Hall. The two seem to have agreed that if the mines could be linked by canal to Manchester, transport costs would be so low that the Duke would be able to undercut all opposition by a considerable and irresistable margin. This must have appealed to the Duke's gambling nature which may have been abandoned but cannot have been forgotten.

John Gilbert was therefore heavily involved in the early planning of the Bridgewater Canal and was also a valued business partner of the Duke. Gilbert's skills in the limestone business enabled him to find substantial volumes of the rock on the Duke's own estates and so improve the fertility and value of his farms. A lead pencil factory was also established at Worsley using plumbago brought down by packhorses from mines near Keswick.

Gilbert also worked on schemes independently of the Duke and it was he who devised schemes for the drainage of Martin Mere near Southport and Chat Moss near Manchester, an expanse of bog later crossed by George and Robert Stephenson's railway line. Gilbert thus deserves to be listed as one of the foremost engineers of his age as well as a very able land agent in the employ of the Duke of Bridgewater.

Time and time again as we journey along the Bridgewater Canal, Gilbert's engineering contributions and financial influence will become evident. These three kings of the Canal Age should perhaps be best considered as a combination of kings and the three wise men — the Duke brought capital, Brindley brought bravery and innovation whilst Gilbert brought business acumen, common sense and considerable engineering skills.

CHAPTER THREE

From Pennington Flash to Worsley Old Hall

THE PRESENT authors are well aware that Pennington can easily be regarded as lying close to and therefore described as a section of the Leeds to Liverpool Canal. Careful examination of archive material, however, proves that the two canals do actually meet at Leigh. This old coal mining area should therefore be considered as the start of the Bridgewater. In 1795, the Duke was granted an Act of Parliament to extend his canal from Worsley to Leigh, there to join what was then known as the Wigan branch of the Leeds and Liverpool Canal. This stretch provided the final inland waterway link between industrial Lancashire and the Midlands via the Cheshire Ring of canals.

The Lancashire coalfield around Leigh had already been exploited for many years but drainage was always a problem especially as more and more coal was extracted. As early as the 17th century, inventors were wondering how to improve the pumping and ventilation of the mines in order to win more and more coal from deeper and deeper levels. In the early days of the canal, coal was brought up from the mines by ponies which pulled bogies. "Trains" of these bogies were directed along wooden rails leading to the canal. Transport to industrial areas was then easily and inexpensively moved along the inland waterway.

The Duke of Bridgewater would have been very familiar with these wagon-trains and wooden railways. Never slow to appreciate new inventions, the Duke saw the threat of railways and some, including the Duke himself, were already suggesting that steam was likely to be the power source of the future.

Thomas Newcomen's atmospheric steam engine was in widespread use but it was far too large, heavy and cumbersome to be any threat to living horse power. James Watt, however, refined the Newcomen engine to produce a high pressure steam boiler. This provided the spur for many inventors and engineers who produced a variety of designs which eventually led to linking the steam to pistons which turned wheels. In the context of the Bridgewater Canal we should not forget that Gilbert had been apprenticed to the Bolton company which built powerful steam engines.

Birds of Pennington Flash — Jay.

First the canal, then the railway, both coupled with improved drainage and pumping led to the mines in the Bickershaw area becoming some of Britain's most productive collieries. The area now known as the 'Flashes' were first mentioned by name on the Ordnance Survey Map of 1892 and were set among arable land and surrounded by a network of railways and, of course, the canal. An overprint carried the words "liable to flooding".

Pennington, however, remained largely rural until the early 1900s but the colliery was increasing in size all the time. Rail and canal links were busy carrying away the coal and the extraction of the mineral was leading to more and more subsidence. Flooding was a continual problem and even caused some concern as shafts penetrated beneath the line of the canal and were deemed to be a potential threat.

By the 1950s, the coal seams were showing signs of exhaustion and the flooded flashes were increasing in size. Local politicians were divided, more by conviction than along party lines, regarding the action which needed to be taken. Should the flashes be filled in and stabilised or should the cheaper and ecologically more sensible alternative be taken by creating a country park based on a lake?

Fortunately, the latter view prevailed and local naturalists, anglers and boaters were consulted making the early 1970s exciting times. We made several visits to the flashes during this period and we scrambled over dirty dumps of coal mining spoil and returned home black from head to foot, but delighted with the impressive list of birds we had seen. Pennington was then in need of landscaping and sensible management. Salvation was at hand

following the 1974 re-organisation of council boundaries. Wigan and Greater Manchester Councils and the newly created North West Water Authority (now privatised as North West Water) drew up a joint plan to create a properly planned nature reserve but developing an acceptable balance between the needs of water sports and wildlife. Trees were planted to stabilise the coal spoil heaps and field vegetation was allowed to grow naturally over the surfaces. The temptation to move too quickly and thus produce an artificial environment was wisely resisted. Many of the plants found here were initially brought as seeds on the feet and feathers of birds.

Pennington Flash was always a friendly place easily accessible to naturalists, but things improved first in 1978 when it was given Country Park status and especially in 1981 when a Ranger Service was established. A small information centre, bird hides throughout the year and free of charge, a nine hole golf course, a picnic site and marked walks have all been provided.

There is ample parking on a pay and display area and Pennington Flash is fast becoming a major birdwatching area which is home to many common species, but which is always likely to turn up a rarity which sets the ornithological world alight. The Country Park has made the maximum use of all its natural assets except one — the canal is almost always ignored. The views from the towpath down over the flashes are magnificent.

Well established breeding birds on and around the flashes include mute swans, tufted duck, mallard, shoveler, gadwall and ruddy duck. This is an impressive list and owes its success to a series of sensitive wardens who have managed to control

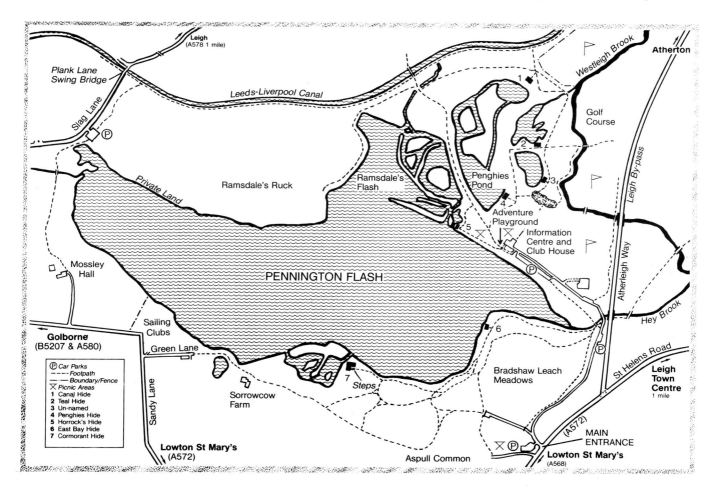

Leigh
(A578 1 mile)

Plank Lane
Swing Bridge

Slag Lane

Leeds-Liverpool Canal

Westleigh Brook

Atherton

Golf
Course

Private Land

Ramsdale's Ruck

Ramsdale's
Flash

Penghies
Pond

Leigh By-pass

1

3

4

Adventure
Playground

5

Information
Centre and
Club House

Mossley
Hall

PENNINGTON FLASH

Atherleigh Way

Hey Brook

Sailing
Clubs

Green Lane

Golborne
(B5207 & A580)

Ⓟ Car Parks
--- Footpath
—·— Boundary/Fence
✕ Picnic Areas
1 Canal Hide
2 Teal Hide
3 Un-named
4 Penghies Hide
5 Horrock's Hide
6 East Bay Hide
7 Cormorant Hide

Sandy Lane

Sorrowcow
Farm

Steps

7

6

Bradshaw Leach
Meadows

St Helens Road

Leigh
Town
Centre
1 mile

Lowton St Mary's
(A572)

Aspull Common

(A572)

MAIN
ENTRANCE

Lowton St Mary's
(A568)

illegal shooting and achieve a balance between boating, angling and the birds' need for space. A few years ago gadwall and ruddy duck were both rare breeders in Britain. The gadwall is native to Britain but the ruddy duck is a North American species which has escaped from captivity and is now becoming a fixture in Britain. Its initial breeding success was in Cheshire and it is in the process of spreading from the meres of that county to other areas. Pennington Flash is really an artificial mere and obviously birds make no distinction — all they care about is the availability of food.

The ruddy duck is a small species measuring only 40 centimetres (16 inches) with the male being easily distinguished by his reddish flanks and back with a blue head and bill plus prominent white cheeks. Even in eclipse plumage this latter feature distinguishes the drake from the duck, as do his long tail feathers. Usually these are held horizontally but during display they are waved about like a banner. The drake can also raise the feathers on his head which then resemble horns, and a specialised air sac in the neck is inflated and a courting tune is played by drumming upon it with his bill. Sometimes the bill is held close to the water and the burping, bubbling call produced is unique to the ruddy duck.

Another fascinating breeding bird of Pennington Flash is the great crested grebe. At the beginning of the 20th century this species was almost extinct. This was due to its attractive plumage which was in great demand by the millinery trade. Kingfishers and jays were also driven to the brink of extinction by the feather trade.

The body of the great crested grebe measures 46 centimetres (18 inches) and the head is carried on a long slender neck. In winter the back is dark grey and the underparts creamy-white. The crown and ear tufts are dark and a line of the eye is clearly visible.

The breeding plumage is splendid and it is easy to see why the Victorian hat makers were prepared to pay high prices for what were called 'grebe skins'. There are long chestnut coloured feathers on the side of the face forming a frill called the tippet and which looks rather like an Elizabethan ruff. This is set off spectacularly against the ear tufts, pink bill and crimson eyes. Both sexes have these assets and use them to maximum effect during the courtship display, which is among the most impressive to be

Birds of Pennington Flash — Shoveler.

seen in the whole of the bird world. The pair dive together, run over the water together and dive for water weed, which they exchange as a sort of engagement present before using it to start building their raft-like nest. Once the nest has been completed, usually by mid-May at Pennington, four chalky white eggs are laid and are incubated by both sexes, a process which occupies them for about a month.

The incubating bird is very wary and whenever

it leaves its eggs it covers them over with weeds. The parents really do take care of their offspring which are striped and are often seen riding around on the backs of the parents. The diet of great crested grebes consists mainly of fish but they also swallow a lot of feathers, including their own. It is thought that the feathers become wrapped around the sharp fish bones and form a pellet. These are regurgitated in the same way that an owl rids itself of sharp bones.

Other breeding species on and around the flashes include little grebe, moorhen, coot, canada goose, partridge, sedge, reed and willow warbler along with an increasing number of birds which use the reeds and the developing woodland areas as roosts.

Birdwatchers find much of interest during the migration periods — in spring there are curlew, common sandpiper, turnstone, little gull and the occasional peregrine falcon, whilst autumn sightings include the increasingly rare merlin and little stint along with huge numbers of fieldfares and redwings.

Many birds on migraton may well use the line of the canal as a navigational aid in much the same way that we use a road map. This is indeed how the canal looks to a bird flying over the area at perhaps 5,000 feet. This is precisely why naturalists who speak so eloquently about the flashes should not fail to appreciate the value of the Bridgewater Canal as a linear nature reserve.

The town of Leigh is often described as a product of the Industrial Age, with muck generated in direct proportion to the brass it accumulated. This does the original settlement something of an injustice because it has a long and not undistinguished history.

In some ways, Leigh anticipated the Industrial Revolution and prepared for the coming of the Bridgewater Canal by exploiting its rich seams of coal from at least the 15th century and possibly even earlier. Mining was thus an important industry, as was the weaving of silk which although it was cottage based, was of considerable importance during the reign of the first Elizabeth. During this period an important livestock and vegetable market was also established.

Also at this time, the parish church of St. Mary the Virgin was an important meeting place as it had been since early medieval times, and probably long before this as the Saxons almost certainly had a church on the site. Little remains today of the medieval building which was, apart from the 15th century tower, largely rebuilt in 1873. The furnishings provide clues to the grandeur of the old church and prominent pieces include a Jacobean chair, an oak reredos wonderfully carved and a fascinating brass memorial on the floor of the north aisle commemorating the life of Henry Travice. Across this gleaming brass 40 poor people were encouraged to step each Maundy Thursday after which they received money accumulated from the interest accrued on a sum of money left in Travice's will.

St Mary's has a firm connection with the Industrial Revolution because it was here in 1761 that Richard Arkwright married Margaret Mullens; neither partner could have realised that his inventions would quickly change the working of first silk and then cotton from a cottage craft into a major industry. You could almost say that King Cotton was crowned in this church. In 1825, Edward Baines in his *Lancashire History* made the valid point that Leigh was "entitled to rank high in the manufacturing annals of Lancashire.

Birds of Pennington Flashes — Moorhen.

It was here that the era of improvements opened."

All writers, including a few "serious" historians, have been known to exercise what is politely termed "poetic licence". We must therefore ask if Baines's view of Leigh can be supported by facts. In this instance it can because as early as 1763, one of the first reliable spinning jennies began to operate in Leigh, and four years later the first functional water frame was constructed in the town. Only one of the original machines is still found in working order and this can be seen in the Mills' Museum at Helmshore.

Leigh was plodding along fluently enough on its own but with the arrival of the canal, and especially when the link between the Bridgewater and the Leeds to Liverpool was opened, the town was catapulted at an alarming rate into the Industrial Age. Out went coal on strings of barges whilst others took away the finished cotton goods; in came raw cotton, lime, stone and bricks. Down came old cottages, up went cathedral-like mills and later their tall chimneys were added, these were originally called 'smoke-pokes', which is a very evocative description.

From Leigh, the canal links to Worsley and passes through Tyldesley and Astley which both benefited from the coming of the smooth aquatic highway. Tyldesley, as a settlement, can also be traced back to Saxon times and like Leigh, cotton spinning and coal mining became its staple industries during the 19th century. Over much of the length of the Bridgewater it is so easy to see only the grubby scars of industry and miss the fact that these are a mere veneer over a rather beautiful rural tapestry.

There were also important coal mines at Astley but, for a time, this was also an important centre for the working of fustian. This is a strong cotton fibre important for the production of clothing and especially furnishings. Corduroy and artificial moleskin are both produced from a fustian base.

From Astley the Bridgewater cuts its way to Worsley, home of the Canal Duke and the womb of the Canal Age.

CHAPTER FOUR

Worsley — the Start of a Great Enterprise

SURROUNDED BY a complex of road junctions around the M61 and M62 motorways is the still delightful village of Worsley looking like a time warp of Tudor England. This is not actually the case but is a rare example of impressive early 20th century planning. A series of surprisingly rural woodland walks strike out from the village and they are a joy to those who have the courage to walk away from the busy roads which have recently divided Worsley into segments.

On one side of the motorway is the parish church of St. Mark and just beyond this is Worsley Old Hall, a still impressive and magnificent half-timbered building set in six acres of fields, trees and outbuildings in various states of repair. In March 1995, the Hall fell on hard times following a successful period as a hotel and restaurant specialising in Jacobean banquets. At the time of writing the Hall is empty.

This was the home of the Duke of Bridgewater during the planning stages of his canal and in its panelled rooms he held discussions with James Brindley and John Gilbert. It is to be hoped that the Hall will soon assume the same or perhaps another useful purpose. The expense would probably be prohibitive but Worsley Old Hall would make a

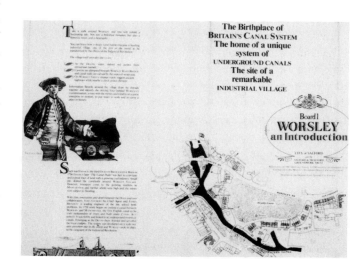

marvellous museum and exhibition centre. Surely Britain's first purpose built canal should be celebrated in some way — and the more impressively this could be done the better it would be.

The Old Hall was a landmark from Elizabethan times and, although some fragments of the original timber framing are still evident, there was some rebuilding during the 18th and 19th centuries. The Duke found his old Hall not totally satisfying and constructed the nearby Red Brick Hall which then became his base during his increasingly regular sojourns at Worsley. The Old Hall, however, was used by his co-workers as a combination of family home and office.

The church of St. Mark would not be recognised by the old Duke as it was rebuilt by the first Earl of Ellesmere in 1846. It is sited on the steep hill called Worsley Brow which then overlooked the village but the view from it now is almost obscured and dominated by the motorway network. It was designed by Sir George Gilbert Scott with the exterior typified by over-ornate gargoyles and crockets. The interior is also crammed with Victorian flamboyance which is somewhat over-exuberant for some. There are, however, many impressive features including the pulpit and organ screens which have been elaborated by the addition of 16th and 17th century panels imported from France and Flanders. Lord Ellesmere's huge and awe inspiring tomb is also a dominant feature of the church interior.

Near to the church, and often missed by visitors in too much of a hurry to spare the time to stop and stare, is one of the entrances to Worsley Woods. Here, bird song can often drown out even the hectic traffic noise of the motorway and the heady scent

Boats have always been busy around the canal at Worsley.

of bluebells can usually swamp the acrid stench of diesel and petrol fumes. The woods were also largely the creation of the First Lord Ellesmere, who even then realised the importance of conservation. He replaced old and fallen trees during an extensive period of planting at which time he had footpaths laid out and ordered the construction of the Old

Warke Dam. This produced an artificial lake which he stocked with fish and close to its banks he constructed a shooting lodge which became known as the aviary.

As Worsley is approached it is worth seeking out the Ellesmere memorial which is often wrongly praised as a monument to Francis Egerton the third Duke of Bridgewater and ace canal builder. It was, in fact, erected in 1859 to celebrate the life of the later Francis Egerton who became the First Earl of Ellesmere. This mock Gothic spike is fringed by trees and is now surrounded by private housing and cannot be easily approached or seen in its original rural tranquility. This is a great pity although a pair of binoculars can be useful.

After the death of the Canal Duke, his will decreed that his estates should pass to Francis Leverson-Gower the second son of the Marquis of Stafford but only if he changed his name to Egerton. Perhaps the Canal Duke still felt that he should have married either of his fiancées and produced his own heir to carry on his name. The 'new' Francis was much loved and in 1846 he was made the Earl of Ellesmere, and throughout his tenure at Worsley he gave generously to the poor, embellished his inheritance and thoroughly deserved his monument. The first Duke deserved his canal as a monument and the first Earl equally deserves this memorial in the woods. The Worsley and Bridgewater Canal complex which we see today are due to both these energetic and able Francis Egertons.

Standing in the village itself and looking at the now closed off entrance to the coal mine canal it is easy to assume that this was just a straightforward cut through the sandstone rock of Worsley Delph.

This began its working life as a quarry. It was only later that the entrance into the rich coal seams was erected. It is also often assumed that this simple cave system was abandoned when mining ceased and flood waters built up.

The Worsley mine canal was a much more complicated system than that and should be regarded as John Gilbert's masterpiece. It was actually a genuine canal with all the complex, and at that time innovative, technology that this entailed. Gilbert's canal was actually longer than the surface cut and some 46 miles of waterway ran off towards coal seams which penetrated beneath Farnworth and almost as far as Bolton.

In one sense, the mine canal was the answer to any engineer's prayer. Drainage was always a problem in a coal mine — in this case, however, all that had to be done was to drain off the water from the mines and into the surface canal.

Most mines also had a logistics problem in getting the coal from the cutting face to the pit head. This usually involved filling bogeys which were then pushed along wooden rails by children or dragged by pit ponies to the shaft. The load was lifted to the surface in large buckets. This was the proceedure employed in the Leigh mines around Pennington.

At Worsley, coal was loaded into simple boats and then propelled by "leggers" who pushed against the walls and the roof of the canal. The coal was thus floated easily, and from the Duke's point of view cheaply, out of the canal and along to the site of the present village green where it was weighed, sold and dispersed. The leggers did not have an easy life and had to be harnessed to the boats to prevent them being knocked overboard during the physically

A bridge close to the old mine workings at Worsley.

demanding journey along the roughly hewn tunnels with numerous rocky edges. They must have been soaking wet during their working day as the tunnels would have been dripping with condensation.

The barges were built as cheaply as possible and were little more than "skeletons" of timber which led to them being christened "starvation boats" by the locals. It was from this primitive design that the long narrow boats typical of canals were later evolved. Examples of starvation boats can still be seen submerged beneath the rusty looking waters at the mine entrance. If ever a museum evolved here one of these could easily be removed from its watery grave, restored and used as an exhibit.

Work on the underground canal started at the same time as the "Main Line Bridgewater". In the former, two separate levels were eventually produced which were linked by an "inclined plane". This had a gradient of 1–in–4 and followed the line of a natural fault in the limestone rock; the use of this geological feature was yet another example of Gilbert's talent as an innovator with a wary eye always on his master's purse strings.

Two locks were built at either end of the inclined plane. A loaded boat entered the top lock and as the water left this lock the starvation boat was settled into an iron cradle. An empty boat was then manouvered into the lower lock. The weight of the full boat coming down the inclined plane raised the empty boat to the upper level.

The inclined plane was a major engineering enterprise in its own right being 138 metres (453 feet) long and 18.2 metres (60 feet) wide. Each cradle was 9.1 metres (30 feet) long and weighed 5080 kg (5 tons) empty. An empty "starvation boat" could weigh up to 4064 kg (4 tons) and carry a load of around 12,192 kg (12 tons) of coal. Each operation of the inclined plane system took 15 minutes and it was estimated that the system could deliver 335,600 kg (350 tons) of coal to the Worsley yards during the course of an eight hour shift.

Whilst drainage was never a problem at Worsley it did have the other hazard feared by all coal miners — the build up of methane gas. This John Gilbert overcame by the construction of a number of ventilation shafts, three of which still exist, and the whole system continued to function effectively until stocks of coal were reduced to uneconomic levels during the late 19th century. Only a well designed system could have continued to function for so long.

The water, now emerging through a metal grill which seals the mine canal entrance, is so rich in iron salts that the minute it is exposed to the air it oxidises and looks like liquid rust. This leads many visitors to utter the word "pollution" with an air of disgust and take no further interest in the whole of the Bridgewater corridor. The seepage of iron salts is typical of all old mine workings and even in some "natural" rocks which contain iron deposits. Most coal deposits are found close to rocks containing iron.

The water, however, is not poisonous and the canal is rich in wildlife from Worsley and along its whole length. Three angling clubs with a total membership of around 20,000 use the canal by permission of the present owners who are The Manchester Ship Canal Company. The clubs ensure that fish stocks are maintained and keep the canal supplied with roach, bream, perch, tench, chub and both common and mirror carp. There are plenty of aquatic plants and animals for fish and aquatic insects to feed upon and these also ensure a healthy population of birds.

Worsley has so many fine looking buildings that it is hard to realise that the village was once one of the largest and busiest industrial complexes in Europe. The now attractive "village green" has been constructed on top of the mine works' yard. The fountain is the base of a red brick chimney which has been preserved as a memorial to the work and energy of the Duke of Bridgewater. It bears a Latin inscription which is roughly translated as follows:-

"A lofty column breathing smoke and fire
Did I the builders glory once inspire
Whose founder was the Duke who far and wide
Bridged water through Bridgewater's countryside.

Stranger, this spot where once did never cease
Great Vulcan's year, who sleep in silent peace
But beneath my very stories does mount
That water's source, his honours spring and fount

Alas that I who gazed o'er field and town
Should to these base proportions dwindle down
But all's not over, still enough remains
To testify past glories, duties place.

The green now looks wonderful and is overlooked by mock Tudor houses built just after 1900. These replaced the warehouses and offices, plus the hovels in which lived the men, women and children who operated the mines and those who worked on the surface and service industries including blacksmiths, carpenters, bricklayers, boatbuilders and those who looked after the hundreds of horses.

We should discount at this point the over-dramatic stories of an overbearing master exploiting the poor. The Duke of Bridgewater risked his whole fortune on the success of his canal and mines and was for a long time in danger of bankruptcy as his finances were stretched almost to breaking point. Despite this, he paid wages, contractors and merchants and only when the canal had been running for some time did the Duke break even. He was not a rich man until a few years prior to his death. In the context of the age in which he lived the Duke was a very good employer.

The canal at Worsley is overlooked by a number of splendid buildings, the most impressive of which is the half-timbered Packet House which some still confuse with Worsley Old Hall. The Packet House was built in the late 18th century as a number of separate buildings. In 1845, the Tudor frontage linking the whole block was added under the influence of the Earl of Ellesmere. This provided some beauty to what had become an industrialised landscape. From the steps in front of the building travellers gathered to board the packet boat which conveyed them in comfort to Manchester, Warrington and Runcorn. In some ways this anticipated Worsley's later function as a dormitory village for those who worked in Manchester. Nearby is an old nailmaker's workshop built in 1725 which therefore pre-dates the canal, and is a welcome reminder of pre Bridgewater Worsley.

Another mock-Tudor building is the Court House, a grade two listed building now situated between the canal and the busy road roundabout which allows access to the motorway. This was also built at the instigation of the Earl of Ellesmere and it was originally the Court Leet and the village hall. It was built on the site of the village stocks, later functioned as the Magistrates Court, and is now a catering establishment.

There is an attractive canalside walk which passes alongside a large flotilla of pleasure craft and on the opposite side of the cut are the historic boatyards. These were built in the 1760s and have changed very little since. The yards are the oldest such buildings still in use in England. The Worsley Dry Docks Limited is now run as a private company and we talked to the directors John Perry and Marilyn Freear. The concept of the modern yard is that the company will hire out the dry docks to the owners of canal craft who can then do their own maintenance and simple repairs. The company can provide the telephone numbers of specialists who are willing to undertake the more major repairs.

Marilyn Freear, who is a canal fanatic, told us that these Worsley Docks played a major role, although this is not always realised, in the history of steamboat technology. Here was built the first experimental steam vessel which also featured the first attempt at the production of the screw propeller. This was in 1799 and had other events not overtaken him the Duke of Bridgewater may well have placed Worsley on the world map as the site of the construction of the world's first operational steamboat.

What a list this would have made; John Gilbert's underground canal, the Duke's steamship and further along the cut towards Manchester the first canal aqueduct in Britain and one of James Brindley's masterpieces.

*'Utopia' is the perfect name for a vessel on **the Bridgewater**.*

Worsley is slowly but surely becoming a tourist centre and, although obviously dominated by the canal, there are other attractions including Wardley Hall, which is yet another building often confused with the Duke's Old Hall. This was built in the early 16th century and more of its original timbering remains than is the case at Worsley Old Hall. It had an inner courtyard and was sheltered behind a moat. A brick range and gatehouse were added to the northerly portion of the Hall in 1652, the whole complex now being the residence of the Roman Catholic Bishop of Salford.

Here resides the skull of Ambrose Barlow a 17th century priest who was created a Saint by order of Pope Paul VI as late as 1970. Father Ambrose was born at Barlow Hall and was such a staunch and true Catholic at a time when, if caught celebrating the mass, there could only be one end for him — death as a martyr. There were many faithful Catholics always willing to risk their own lives by sheltering their priests. One such faithful was the Downes household who resided at Wardley Hall.

Ambrose Barlow was admitted to the priesthood in 1604, a terrifying period during which James I was almost paranoic in his fear of a Papist plot. Who could blame him as in 1605 Guy Fawkes and the Gunpowder ploters almost blew him and his Parliament into the next world?

Father Ambrose administered to the Lancashire faithful who hid him in cunningly located secret rooms called priest holes which were a feature of Catholic owned houses throughout the 16th and 17th centuries. On Easter Sunday, 1641, the luck which had followed Father Ambrose for so long finally ran out — he was betrayed and was captured after he had forbidden his flock to protect him by force of arms.

The fiercely Puritan vicar of Leigh arrived at the head of a group of fired up Protestants and dragged Father Ambrose to Winwick. Whilst being kept closely confined here he suffered a stroke. Despite his very obvious fraility, the climate of the time allowed the Papists no mercy and he was sent off to Lancaster Castle where he languished for more than four months before being brought to trial. Trial is perhaps the wrong word for his fate was sealed long before his appearance in front of the fiercely biased Protestant judges. He was quickly sentenced to death and dragged to the gallows feet first and strapped to a hurdle. There he was hanged, cut down before he was dead, disembowelled, probably castrated and his body cut into quarters. His friends, including Francis Downes of Wardley Hall, never deserted their priest. They watched his execution and even managed to obtain Father Ambrose's head which they carried in secret back to Wardley where it has remained ever since.

The Downes family well knew the risks involved in harbouring such a sacred relic — they could well have been executed themselves. They therefore resorted to subterfuge by weaving a legend around the skull, which has occasionally led writers of popular histories to confuse fact with a carefully invented fiction.

The family insisted that the head was that of Roger Downes, their black sheep of a son, who died during a drunken brawl in London during which he killed a man before himself being hacked down. His skull was brought home for burial. Nobody seemed to ask why all the young man's body was not brought home but the head story was accepted. This was only proved false in 1780 when a family vault in Wigan Parish Church was opened. The complete skeleton of Reckless Roger was discovered with his skull still attached to his body although showing the effects of the fatal blow. Part of the cranium was sawn across, probably being a crude attempt at an autopsy. Roger's body was probably taken to Wigan because it was then far enough from Wardley to make the connection with Father Ambrose difficult to establish.

This would seem to indicate that the skull still kept in a niche of the Wardley Hall staircase is indeed that of Father Ambrose Barlow. The skull has had several adventures having survived being buried, partly dismembered and even on one occasion thrown into the moat. Any disturbance has always been followed by violent storms and catastrophes so that it is now deemed wiser to let this turbulent priest remain in peace in the bosom of the family who remained as faithful to their confessor as he had been to them.

The Worsley area has thus a justified claim to be on the tourist trail — here is an irresistable combination of history — political, industrial and natural. From its very beginning the Bridgewater Canal is a fascinating ribbon of English political and social history and one which continues to delight us as we follow it towards Manchester.

CHAPTER FIVE

Worsley to Manchester via Barton & Trafford Park

T HIS SECTION of the Bridgewater Canal, like most of the others, brings the most rewards to those who are prepared to explore on foot. From Worsley the towpath leads past Alder Forest towards Monton and then skirts Ellesmere Park before continuing under the motorway to Patricroft and the famous Barton Aqueduct at Eccles.

Alder Forest now long buried beneath the urban sprawl was once just that — a damp woodland dominated by alder trees. Few British trees have been so useful as the alder, the timber of which was used to produce gates, posts and the soles of clogs. It is the only British tree which can exist with its roots always waterlogged. Even willow cannot survive when all its nutrients are leached out. Alder, like the pea family, has nodules in its roots. These contain a bacteria which can convert atmospheric nitrogen into nitrates and can therefore survive in areas where water has washed away all the nutrients. Because alder timber is part in water and partly in drier areas it does not seem to warp. Alder forests

were therefore economically important as clogs could be made to measure from its timber and last for years without losing their shape. Many of Manchester textile workers' clogs were made in the

The first Barton Aquaduct, built in 1761 and Brindley's masterpiece as it crossed the Irwell. It was replaced in 1893 as the Manchester Ship Canal needed more space.

area between Worsley and the existing town.

Our canal journey continues through the now bewildering industrial sprawl (thank goodness for a towpath to follow!) to the well named Watermeetings at Stretford. The main line then heads into Cheshire, but in this chapter we divert to the left along the branch leading into the centre of Manchester. Obviously, the Duke of Bridgewater aimed at Manchester and did not initially envisage a link via the Rochdale Canal, leading over the Pennines and into Yorkshire but this soon evolved and the two inland waterways were largely instrumental in making Manchester prosperous.

Eccles was absorbed as an industrial suburb of Manchester largely because of the construction of the Bridgewater Canal. Part of the story of this development is told in the Museum of Mining within Buile Hill Park. Mining for coal in Eccles is explained by the use of models of drift and deep shafted pits. There is also a more general display of mining techniques, tools and history all housed within a splendid building designed in 1827 by Sir Charles Barry.

At Monks Hall Museum, which has been run by Salford Corporation since 1961, there is a more general display of the industrial development of the area, with the centre of attraction being the machinery removed from James Nasmyth's Bridgewater foundry which was built, for obvious reasons, alongside the canal at Patricroft in 1836. Nasmyth was yet another in a long line in Scots engineers of real genius and he invented the steam hammer which enabled him to fashion his products much more quickly and more economically than his rivals.

Monks Hall itself can be confusing because it has a Victorian mock-Tudor frontage. Why this was added is something of a mystery because the original hall is actually a 16th century timber framed house of considerable architectural merit. It is seen at its best from the back garden which is hidden behind a high wall. For many years the hall was a country farmhouse, later swamped by the buildings associated with the Industrial Revolution.

Even older than Monks Hall is St Mary's parish church. The present structure is Norman but it was savagely restored in 1862. Most historians accept that there was a settlement here in Saxon times. The word Eccles (from which we also get the word ecclesiastical) is said to derive from the Celtic word for a church. This suggests that missionaries to the Saxons may have converted "the heathen" in these parts. In its days as a dominant country parish, it is likely that Eccles had more influence over the area than the parish church of the one time village of Manchester and which is now the cathedral. The interior contains a pre-Conquest cross and the solid oak south door dates to the 14th century, as does the Boothe chantry chapel, whilst there is also some 16th century Flemish glass.

Once the Bridgewater Canal provided a cheap corridor to lucrative markets from the early 1760s, industries evolved at speed. First came silk spinning and weaving but these were soon overtaken by the working of the newly imported cotton, which was perfectly suited to the moist climate of the area. Later came the manufacture of machine tools and then steam locomotives; the first motor-driven fire engine was, in fact, built in Eccles and it was also the birthplace of the pioneer aircraft builder Sir Allick Verdan-Rol. The name of Eccles will be forever remembered in the name of a cake made from butter

The Barton Swing Aqueduct — a remarkable feat of engineering.

and currants. A shop in Church Street still follows the original recipe. The shop was rebuilt in the 19th century on the site where the cake was first made. This was Ye Olde Thatch said to have been built in 1094.

After the Bridgewater came the Manchester Ship Canal, whilst at Barton the innovations continued into the modern era with the establishment of the first municipal airport. This now continues to operate on a small and largely unnoticed scale, leaving the Barton Aqueduct to carry the name of Eccles into the history books.

The Barton Aqueduct at work.

Canal historians point to the Barton Aqueduct as being one of the seven wonders of the Canal Age. Far too many people then point to James Brindley as its architect. The present structure is a much more modern marvel built to replace Brindley's aqueduct which was opened in 1770 to carry the Bridgewater Canal over the river Irwell. The opening of Brindley's Barton Aqueduct was spectacular and described in euphoric terms by the correspondent of the *Manchester Mercury*.

"On Friday last his Grace the Duke of Bridgewater with the Earl of Stamford and several other gentlemen, came to Barton to see the water turned into the canal over the river Irwell, which drew together a large number of spectators and it is with pleasure that we can inform the public that the experience answered the most sanguine expectations of everyone present. As soon as the water had risen to the level of the canal a large boat carrying upwards of 50 tons was towed along the new part of the canal over arches across the river Irwell which were so firm, secure and compact that not a single drop of water could be perceived to ouse thro' any of them, although the surface of the canal is 38 feet above the navigable river under it. The canal will be carried to Manchester with all expedition and we are creditably informed will be completed before Lady Day next, every seeming difficulty being now removed, and that in the meantime the subterraneous Navigation to the Collieries will be perfected so that we may expect to have a supply of coals as will reduce considerably the price of coal to the consumer and this work will be of very great use as well as ornament to the town of Manchester."

The correspondent of the *Manchester Mercury*

made the point that Brindley's aqueduct did not leak. This was due to the engineers "invention" of the process later called 'puddling'. This involved pressing down wet mud into the bed of the canal and then compressing it still further using feet and flat pieces of timber. Layer upon layer of this mud produced a waterproof foundation. Ever after this process was an accepted part of canal construction.

When the Irwell was incorporated into the Manchester Ship Canal in 1890, Brindley's structure was found to be too low to allow the masts of large ocean going vessels to pass beneath it. There was nothing for it but to remove the stone masterpiece and replace it with an even more ambitious project.

The Bridgewater Canal itself could obviously not be raised and the only solution was to construct a swing aqueduct which carried the water actually within it. Many have heard or read about the engineering wonders of the Barton Aqueduct but far too few take the trouble to travel to see it. Whilst the new aqueduct was being built, the extensive excavations unearthed a prehistoric "dug out" canoe.

The "modern" aqueduct is unique in that it carried one canal (the Bridgewater) over another (the Manchester Ship). The moveable section is a 100 metres (330 feet) long steel section swinging on a central pivot and when the Bridgewater aqueduct is in operation huge rubber coated wedges push hard together to form watertight joints. The system of gates can be opened when there are no vessels passing along the Ship Canal to allow the Bridge-water to function as a "normal canal". Although nowhere nearly so busy as in the past, the Ship Canal remains an important waterway and the Barton Swing Aqueduct therefore still needs to be manned

During excavations for the New Barton swing aqueduct carrying the Bridgewater Canal over the Manchester Ship Canal in 1890.

and maintained. Its operators must have been busy in the early years of the 20th century when both canals were well used and important waterways.

It can fairly be said that the Bridgewater Canal brought industry to Eccles but it was the Manchester Ship Canal which was the main cause of the swamping of the rural Trafford Park beneath a forest of engineering and industrial complexes. Any student of Industrial Estates must first study Trafford Park, some 2,000 acres, inside which the first attempt at industrial planning in the world took place.

Before the Bridgewater Canal was constructed Trafford Park stood in splendid isolation with the nearest watercourse being the Irwell. The name Trafford means the "road across the ford" and obviously related to the area of relative shallow water across the river.

The Trafford family were of ancient lineage being Saxons with large estates granted before the Norman Conquest by King Canute to Ralph or Randolphus of Trafford. The Traffords were one of the few Saxons to hold on to their inheritance following William the Conqueror's defeat of Harold's army at Hastings and they assumed the Norman name of de Trafford. The Irwell was important to the manor because of its rich supply of fish, especially salmon which migrated up the Mersey and spawned in the upper reaches of its tributaries including the Irwell.

No doubt there was a manor house on the site from at least the 11th century but at the time of the cutting of the Bridgewater the mansion on site was a Tudor half timbered structure similar to others in Lancashire, such as Ordsall (also near the banks of the Irwell) and Speke on the Mersey.

The de Traffords did not welcome the Bridgewater Canal and refused point blank to allow the Duke to impinge upon their estate. The line of the canal could therefore not be direct and had to skirt around Trafford Park. The original residence stood near Trafford Bar and the new canal actually sliced between the house and the river, an area not controlled by the de Traffords, much to their dismay. They abandoned their Tudor House in consequence and built a splendid new residence close to Wiggleswick, near Barton, but secreted it behind extensive woodlands well within the grounds of Trafford Park. Those who wish to visualise what the scene was like in these days should visit Lyme Park, Tatton

or especially Dunham Massey which actually survived the coming of the canal.

The pure line of the de Trafford's family can be traced from Canute's time up until 1779 when Humphrey de Trafford died but left no children to inherit the lands and to carry on their traditions. The estate was then given over to a nephew who moved into the new residence. He established his line which lived in relative peace **with the Bridgewater** which attracted industry around **the canal** but obviously not within the park itself.

The family were, however, further angered by the coming of the next canal in the 1890s. The Manchester Ship Canal, in the region of Trafford Park, absorbed the river Irwell and the estate was now hemmed in by artificial and increasingly busy waterways. Sir Humphrey Francis de Trafford, once he realised he could not prevent the construction of the Ship Canal, decided to leave his estate. Speculation mounted that Trafford Park was about to be sold to the Manchester Corporation and developed as a recreation area for the local workers. Industrialists, however, also had their eyes on this prime site which was so well supplied with working waterways.

In the end Sir Humphrey sold his estate, of almost 1200 acres, not as anticipated to the Ship Canal Company or to Manchester Corporation but to E.T. Hooley whose initial intention was to construct a susbstantial pleasure park to rival Belle View or even Blackpool.

There are few people more determined, or perhaps devious within the law is a better phrase, than experienced industrialists. At this time, a major role was played by Marshall Stevens who was the first

General Manager of the Ship Canal. In 1896, he formed the Trafford Park Estates Company and persuaded E.T. Hooley to sell his recently acquired and much sought after estate. He was no doubt happy to have made such a quick and substantial profit. The Company paid £650,000 which was almost twice the sum he had paid for it.

Marshall Stevens' original plan was to develop the site as a sophisticated combination of an industrial and leisure complex but the end result was a heavy and eventually total concentration upon the former. It was originally planned to develop the hall as a residential hotel with an attached golf course with its lake stocked with fish. Perhaps the construction of a racecourse was a little ambitious but, otherwise, these plans of the 1890s hardly differ from many schemes regarding other rural estates being placed before the planning authorities a full century later.

Muck in those days generated brass and in less than 20 years Trafford Park was the most famous industrial estate in the world and the first to be purpose built.

The estate was able to develop so quickly during this period because of what were then a unique combination of factors. Firstly, the Bridgewater and then the Manchester Ship Canal provided a reliable link to the sea which modern day industrialists would call the essential infrastructure. Secondly, the Trafford Park site was obviously undeveloped which allowed for easy planning of the factories. The only compulsory purchase order was the original take over of the estate. Thirdly, the whole complex was close enough to Salford and Manchester to provide, initially at least, a readily available and eager workforce.

Progress is, however, always slow without a massive injection of capital. No doubt because of its easy links with the sea Trafford Park mushroomed, but it did have an impressive and irresistible injection

Coal barges hard at work discharging coal from the canal to Trafford Park power station.

of American cash and this was accompanied by their associated aggressive marketing techniques.

George Westinghouse, a giant in the field of Electrical Engineering in the States, initially tried to use local contractors, but they were not used to working as quickly as he demanded. George therefore turned to James C. Stewart who swept in like a whirlwind and from the start of the Trafford Enterprise in 1901, he had thousands of men hard at work within weeks. Soon, what amounted to a mini-city developed between the Bridgewater and the Ship Canal. Houses, libraries and schools drew in workers and other industries were not slow to realise the potential. The idea of Trafford Park in the literal sense of the word had vanished within a couple of years of this enterprise starting.

The British Electric Car Company moved into the site but was soon taken over by Henry Ford, who operated out of Trafford Park until the 1930s. The original automobile works were later adapted for the construction of Merlin Aero engines which were so vital during the Second World War. Also geared to the war effort was a huge Metro-Vickers complex producing first Manchester and later Lancaster bombers. Trafford Park already had an impressive pedigree in the aviation field as Manchester's first commercial aerodrome was developed here in 1911 but later the runway space demanded by this industry was not economical.

The Park also saw early attempts at commercial radio broadcasting which began in May 1922 and thus predated the BBC — indeed, industrialists from Trafford Park were part of the BBC's initiation team.

To list the industries of Trafford Park would be tedious but Kilvert's Lard and Kellogg cereals must be mentioned. The area had its own rail, tram, and later, bus services and a workforce which was to some extent insular and fiercely proud of its newly acquired fame. This feeling is still apparent in the support given to Manchester United Football Club and to a lesser extent the County Cricket Club. They are both based in the conurbation of New Trafford but their grounds are called Old Trafford and thus continue a family name which takes us back to the days before William the Conqueror came to England. These are among the few areas of greenery remaining in the Trafford Park area.

When we see what happened to Trafford Park following the cutting of the Bridgewater Canal it is easy to see why the families in other stately homes such as Dunham Massey and Norton Priory did not sleep easily in their beds.

In Stretford stands the Watch House Inn which was in use long before the construction of the canal or the hotel. It was occupied by lookouts whose job was to keep a wary eye on the levels of the Mersey and to give warning whenever flooding was imminent.

In this chapter, however, we will leave the main line of the Bridgewater and follow a branch which cuts into the heart of Manchester.

The area of central Manchester known as Castlefield has had a chequered career but has been at the centre of events since Roman times. During the Canal Age it was the life-blood of Manchester. This was followed by a period of neglect and dereliction, but now tourism has taken over and Castlefield is once again dominant and mightily impressive.

The name derives from a large complex of ruins which constituted a Roman fort and the associated buildings which were not finally submerged by a mass of buildings until the 18th century. The construction of first the Bridgewater and then the Rochdale Canal led to the dismantling of the fort. All remnants finally disappeared only as the railway network was driven into the heart of the area with the intention of absorbing the trade formerly the monopoly of the canal company.

The name Manchester (like Chester and Ribchester) indicates the presence of a Roman fort. The first structure has been dated to around AD 79 and was constructed of wood. This must have been successful as a second fort was built of stone and protected by ditches, some of which have now been excavated. The third and fourth forts were considerably larger and were garrisoned by both infantry and cavalry. The reconstructions we can see now were those operating from AD 200 until AD 410 when the Romans departed to protect their native city from the invading heathen tribes. Near to the Gatehouse are murals painted on the walls showing the Roman legions.

Castlefield was just that in medieval Manchester — it was a castle in the fields. Another nearby area of interest is Camp Field and in 1800 this was right on the edge of Manchester. In 1761, what became known as the Knott Mill Fair was established to celebrate the opening of the Bridgewater Canal and became an annual event during the Easter period. Bare knuckle boxing, waxworks, lion taming, fat men, whiskered women and assorted freaks were all on view and drinking and violence typified the fair. Things became so bad that in 1876 the Knott Mill fair was abolished.

Knott is an old English word meaning a bunch of flowers and Castlefields must have been rich in plants

until Manchester's growth eventually swamped it. Near the reconstructed Roman gatehouse a garden has been established in which plants cultivated by the Romans have been planted. These they used for food and for medicinal use. The list of plants include sweet chestnut, walnut, fig, mulberry, medlar, bullace (which were related to plums and damsons), cherry, crab apple and pear. There are also pot herbs such as sage, fennel, marjoram, rosemary and bay. Many garden plants which we now take for granted were introduced to Britain by the Romans. They also made use of native plants, attractive in all seasons but particularly in autumn. The red rose hips were thought to be "healthy" in Roman times. We now know that they were right as the hips are a rich source of Vitamin C. The whole of this area was established as the very first Urban Heritage Park in 1982 and has gone from strength to strength ever since.

In the early 19th century the Castle-in-the-Fields was still a rural hamlet on the outskirts of Manchester, but with the canal basin becoming ever larger, more important and therefore more intrusive. In recent times extensive and expensive improvements have taken place and visitors can now visit a reconstruction of the fort and the walls which protected it. The site is carefully signed and there is a Visitors' Centre situated between the canal basin and the Museum of Science and Industry which is also relevant to those interested in the history of inland waterways. Quite naturally most tourists are interested in Roman Manchester but increasing numbers follow the directions from the fort, beneath the railway arches to the Castlefield Basin. Here is the junction of the Bridgewater Canal with the Rochdale Canal which then strikes its way out through the heart of the

Coal barges hard at work discharging coal from the canal to Trafford Park power station.

city and onwards to Todmorden into Yorkshire, through Hebden Bridge to Sowerby Bridge where it links into the Aire Calder Navigation. This navigation provides access to the Humber estuary. Here then was another vital cross-Pennine link which is gradually being reconstituted.

The Rochdale link was completed in Trafalgar year of 1805 and extended its former terminus at the Dale Street Basin near Piccadilly to the Bridgewater at Castlefields which gave the inland towns of the Pennines a westward link to the sea and the American market. Vital raw cotton could now reach Rochdale and Oldham.

The Duke's Bridgewater scheme reached Manchester and the first wharf was built at Castlefield in 1765. The original buildings have gone but there is a fine example of an early 19th century brick and timber warehouse. Completed in 1827 the Merchants Warehouse, as it is known, is an architectural triumph, a blend of structure fitted to function, but also an equally splendid combination of art and science. The most interesting features are small semi-circular windows as well as two apertures known as shipping holes set on the wall closest to the canal and through which merchandise could be lifted by means of block and tackle from barges and then wheeled to their allotted storage space.

The Middle Warehouse was built around the same time and beyond the railway viaducts are the remnants of old branches of the canal which once linked to the now demolished Staffordshire warehouse and also to another Brindley masterpiece which became known as the Giant's Basin. The function of this basin was to carry surplus and potentially dangerous water away from the canal frontage and down into the river Medlock.

The Castlefield complex did not just spread in one direction but also extended along Castle Street where still stands Gail House, a warehouse dating to the mid-19th century and close to yet another reminder of Brindley's work. This is the Castlefield Coal Wharf which was opened in 1765. In many ways this is the most significant feature of the whole Bridgewater Canal, at least from the Duke's standpoint. His original intention was to transport coal at a competitive price from Worsley to Manchester. With the opening of the Coal Wharf his objective had been realised.

All this canal construction put an almost unbearable strain on the Duke of Bridgewater's finances. He had to find £9000 to purchase the Hulme Hall estates which occupied the ground needed for his warehouses and further sums were needed to pay the workforce. He borrowed heavily, sold property, including Bridgewater House in London, and reduced his personal servants to what he considered to be an absolute minimum. He urgently needed income from his enterprise and this began to improve with the completion of the Coal Wharf. A waterwheel began to raise coal from the canal barges at the rate of five tons per hour. As Manchester took advantage of cheap fuel and extended its mills the building industry also benefited. Bricks and lime used to produce mortar arrived via the canal (and later along the Rochdale) which all increased the Duke's revenue.

The history of the area is graphically explained in the Castlefield Visitors' Centre situated in a building, once the Free Library, and which opened in 1882. Regular boat rallies are now held in the basin with the most impressive event being held in early September.

This complex area goes some way to explaining the historical significance of the Duke's canal, and gives an incentive to follow the inland waterways signposts and return to the main line at Stretford and follow the Bridgewater into Cheshire.

CHAPTER SIX

Stretford to Dunham Massey via Sale & the Bollin Aqueduct

A painting by Adriaen Van Diest of Dunham Massey, worked in 1697.

STRETFORD DID HAVE some industry prior to the construction of the canals and by the 14th century it had become famous for the manufacture of woollen products. Those of us who have stood at the Stretford End shouting for United may have difficulty in conjuring up thoughts of a village surrounded by green fields full of sheep; perhaps when we listen to the sound of a cricket ball striking the willow during an Old Trafford Test Match we may find the connection rather more easy to make.

Stretford does, however, still retain one particularly unspoiled reminder of how green its valley once was — this is Longford Park. This consists of some 80 acres of splendour enfolding Longford Hall like a green blanket. This was the one time home of John Rylands who made his fortune in textiles and became such a benefactor to Manchester. The John Rylands library given to the City by his widow is one of the most famous in the world.

The John Rylands library is a veritable treasure trove, and deserves its reputation because of its collection of books with medieval jewelled bindings. John Rylands began his working life in Wigan as a weaver and he, by hard work and great ability, amassed a great fortune. John was a great philanthropist but also used his wealth to build up his library.

Following her husband's death his widow founded a library as a memorial to his name and had a fine neo-Gothic building purpose-built to house the collection. It has been open to the public since 1900 and was designed by Basil Champneys.

It houses the earliest dated print in western Europe which is an image of St. Christopher made in 1423. Also in the library is a Gutenberg Bible and examples of the printers art from all over Europe.

The library also offers facilities for students of Egyptology and archaeology including manuscripts written on clay, bamboo, papyrus and parchment from the third millennium up to the 20th century. Among the 250,000 documents skillfully stored here is a fragment of St. John's Gospel written by a scribe before AD 150.

The library still has funds accumulated from the legacy which allow the collections to be increased and more than half a million pounds was spent on the purchase of the Crawford manuscripts from Earl Spencer's Althorp collection.

From Longford Park the Bridgewater Canal cuts its way through Sale and in doing so writes an impressive chapter on the history of transport. The canal crosses the river Mersey by Barfoot Bridge, which is situated at one extremity of Sale Water Park and then is itself crossed by the busy M63. During the construction of the motorway, gravel was extricated from the area and this was sensibly

Great Crested Grebe.

allowed to flood. It was then landscaped and developed for a number of recreational purposes but with a refreshing emphasis on the wildlife. Here naturalists will be reminded of the fauna and flora of Pennington Flash and on one July day we watched a family of great crested grebes, numerous young moorhens and coots, whilst dragonflies and damselflies seemed to be present in huge numbers. Many of these were mating and the females were laying eggs among the stems of water weeds. Dragonflies are large insects which feed upon other flying insects which they catch in a net-like arrangement created by meshing their front legs to produce a cradle-shaped structure. Dragonflies are just as territorial as birds and can frequently be seen fighting over space. The life of the adults is quite short. Eggs are laid in, or close to, water and the larvae may spend several years as aquatic larvae before emerging as adults, whose function is to breed as quickly as possible. In winter the wildfowl numbers are increasing all the time as the birds learn to recognise the area as a feeding area.

At Sale there was once an influential priory but only gardens now occupy the site. Students of physics should also pay a visit to Sale for here lived James Prescott Joule who worked out the mathematical relationship between heat, work and electrical energy. He is buried in St. Anne's cemetery whilst the house in which he lived still stands and there is a plaque on the wall of the Town Hall celebrating his vital work. Joule was born in Salford and studied in Manchester during the early 19th century. One of his tutors was John Dalton, the discoverer of the Atomic Theory in 1806. In Joule's time, Sale was a country town surrounded by green fields and with no sign of the urban sprawl which has now smothered it, along with other once quiet places such as Altrincham and Chorlton which also now has a water park.

Some idea of what the area was like during the early years of the Bridgewater Canal can be gained by following the beautiful walk along the towpath towards the still magnificent Dunham Massey Hall which was built near the site of a prehistoric burial mound. This is well worth a long visit and is now splendidly and sympathetically administered by the National Trust. The towpath is now part of the Cheshire Ring Walk and marks the point from which the Bridgewater emerges from the cloak of industry into the fresh air and green fields which once typified its whole length.

Dunham Massey's 18th-century frontage is seen at its best when reflected in the limpid waters of its moat and it looks particularly attractive when morning mist rises from its surface.

Dunham's present building began as an Elizabethan mansion centred around two courtyards, one now cobbled and dominated by the buildings which were needed to service what became a very important estate. The other has been converted into a particularly attractive formal garden enfolded around a central fountain.

During the period between 1732 and 1740 the house was extensively restored with much of the original wooden timbering being encased in brick. The new look was designed by John Norris who worked for the eccentric and somewhat irascible George Booth, the second Earl of Warrington. George Booth flew in the face of mid-18th century values by advocating divorce by consent if the two partners (especially the man!) felt that they were incompatible.

John Norris's improvements and extensions to Dunham Massey have stood the test of time, even though it was neglected for many years and another restoration was needed in 1905 when the estate belonged to a descendant of George Booth. This was William Grey who was the Ninth Earl of Stamford. Those who had held the stewardship in the

Elizabethan Watermill at Dunham Massey.

intervening years seem to have done the grand old house few favours. Many of its treasures had been sold and the fabric of the house itself had been neglected.

The essential Edwardian restoration was, on the whole, sensitively done which was not always the hallmark of the architects of a period often typified by over-confidence during the late Victorian period. Many of their so called 'improvements' to medieval buildings were only marginally better than demolition.

William Grey took the best available advice, including that of Percy Macquoid who was a recognised connoisseur of the art of the period, as was the architect J. Compton Hall, and between the three of them a remakably Jacobean feel was given to Dunham Massey. The 10th Earl of Stamford, also named William Grey, and which has obviously led to some confusion, also took a great pride in Dunham Massey and eagerly set about tracing the whereabouts of the original furniture and fittings which had been sold. Wherever possible he purchased them and brought them back to Dunham.

The library is a joy and the 10th Duke's study is particularly impressive, whilst the initially austere looking chapel imparts a very friendly atmosphere, providing the visitor stays in it long enough to get used to it. Close by there is a remarkable space which was once part of the long gallery which was so typical of Tudor Houses. These galleries were used for entertainment during inclement weather and one of the most popular games was bowls. The idea of indoor bowling tournaments is thus much older than modern television audiences realise.

The old gallery at Dunham is now filled by a splendid collection of pictures, among the best of which is Guercino's "Mars, Venus and Cupid with Saturn as time". Of more local interest, however, are commissioned views of the house as it was in the 17th and 18th centuries, including works by Adriaen van Diest, Knyff and John Harris the younger. These all show the expanse of the magnificent grounds, which still give pleasure to visitors, especially those with an interest in natural history.

Pheasants call from the undergrowth, tree creepers, great spotted woodpeckers and the occasional nuthatch climb among the trees and in spring the bird song is wonderful. Medieval landowners maintained a deer park, partly because of their love of hunting but mainly to ensure a supply of fresh meat. Until freezing techniques developed late in the present century, keeping a constant supply of edible meat was not easy and the present herd of fallow deer were bred to provide this need. This species has, however, always been a beautiful addition to the parks of England since the days of the Normans. Some experts think that there were fallow deer in England from Roman times but most think that introductions from around 1150 are much more likely.

The natural sounds of Dunham Massey are all the more impressive to those who walk along the towpath of the Bridgewater Canal because of the startling contrast to the industrial areas which have been seen between Manchester and Dunham. The contrast between this place and the once equally elegant Trafford Park should not be glossed over either.

The residents of Dunham Massey did not welcome the coming of the canal. It disrupted the life in their deer park and disturbed the peace of the nearby river Bollin and its tributaries which ran through the park. Its current powered its watermills, one of which has been recently restored. Furthermore, it brought the rough navvies into contact with the servants, especially the gamekeepers whose stock was poached by the intruders. The comparatively high wages offered to canal labourers may also have tempted the estate workers to change their employment.

No doubt the River Bollin itself was popular with the canal workers as it was rich in fish, especially trout and to a lesser extent salmon. At that time the course of the Bollin had not been affected by artificial watercourses and it meandered on to its junction with the river Mersey. The construction of the Bridgewater Canal did not permanently affect this union apart from the fact that it was carried over the Bollin on an aqueduct.

The huge enterprise of the Manchester Ship Canal, however, was much more intrusive and for a considerable stretch between Irlam and Bollin Point the Ship Canal and the Mersey are now one and the same. It was easier for the canal builders to use a straight stretch of river than to cut a brand new channel. The work, however, did involve cutting off a section of river, the old bed of which is still a damp swamp to this day. Just beyond Warburton the Bollin feeds into the Ship Canal and almost opposite at Bollin Point the Mersey leaves the Ship Canal and flows on its original course towards Warrington.

The Bollin Aqueduct, or rather the problems associated with it, were largely responsible for the setting up of the Bridgewater Canal Trust in 1971.

On the 2nd April 1971, a strident report reached the police in Altrincham that the Bridgewater Canal was beginning to leak from a point close to the

Dunham Massey Kitchen.

Bollin Aqueduct. This carries the canal some 10.4 metres (34 feet) over the valley floor. The water tumbling down from the breach into the river had increased its flow to such an extent that a 27.5 metre (90 foot) wide valley was eroded. The landscape looked as if a huge glacier had just scraped its way down the Bollin valley.

Remedial action was quickly taken with stop logs placed on either side of the breach to prevent any more water from leaking out of the canal. Despite this action the water levels in Manchester, some ten miles away, had fallen by 35 centimetres (14 inches). The problems were particularly severe as the Bridgewater had no locks on its main line and consequently the cumulative pressure of water on the breach was immense.

The damage caused was obviously going to be expensive to repair, especially in the 1970s when the canals were not economically important anymore. They were, however, becoming increasingly valuable as a tourist attraction. In 1968, a Transport Act had

The canal breach in the Lymm-Dunham Massey area. This potentially disastrous event occured in 1971.

been passed to take note of this particular problem. Its terms would have allowed the Manchester Ship Canal Company to have partially closed the Bridgewater Canal by sealing off the two ends of the breach and inserting a metal pipe to carry the water over the problem area. This would have solved the problem of leakage but would obviously not have allowed barges, or even smaller pleasure craft to pass. The Canal Company certainly had no pressing economic incentive to spend the £250,000 needed to repair the breach.

For once, men of business showed commendable common sense and a most sensible attitude to conservation. The idea of setting up a Trust to take responsibility for the maintenance was discussed. The formation of a working party was enough to persuade the Manchester Ship Canal company to repair the breach and the Bridgewater was open again for navigation in September 1973.

By November 1975 the Trust was fully operational and its members then included representatives from Cheshire County Council, Warrington Borough Council, Halton Borough Council, Macclesfield Borough Council, Trafford Borough Council and the City Councils of Manchester and Salford, plus the Wigan Metropolitan Borough Council, and of course, the Manchester Ship Canal Company itself. No praise is too high for the achievements of the Trust which meets every six months. In such capable hands Britain's oldest canal would seem to have an assured future.

From the Bollin Aqueduct the Bridgewater Canal passes Little Bollington, which should not be confused with Bollington, a much more substantial settlement further upstream on the river Bollin and above

Wilmslow. Little Bollington has its own quiet attraction added to by its attractive inn 'The Swan with Two Necks'. Many of England's old inns have this name and their signs usually show two headed swans. The origin is, however, practical rather than mythological and takes us back to the days when mute swans were eaten for food. Any unmarked bird belonged to the monarch who gave permission to others to take a number of birds. Swans were rounded up and their bills marked to indicate who they belonged to. A reminder of this period can still be seen along the Thames which has retained what has become known as the Swan Upping ceremony. Swans given to the Vintners Company could be marked by 'two nicks' and they could serve the birds in their restaurants. Here then we have the 'Swan with two Nicks'. The poetic licence of inn signwriters has led to the name "Swan with two Necks", which are obviously much more easily noticed than two insignificant nicks.

From Bollington a towpath walk leads through a stretch of very pretty countryside and here we once watched a kingfisher successfully diving for fish in the canal. This is always an ideal place to pause for a break, especially in the vicinity of Agden Wharf. There is a splendid stroll from here to Lymm.

CHAPTER SEVEN

Agden Bridge to Stockton Heath via Lymm & Grappenhall

A T AGDEN WHARF is a pleasant little shop which sells provisions to boaters and usually has a good selection of souvenirs and books. Here is yet another stretch of the Bridgewater which is guaranteed to please the naturalist. We once walked this stretch accompanied by a group of schoolchildren who were being introduced to the delights of freshwater ecology. Their collections proved that life in the canal is every bit as fascinating as that found around it. Caddis fly larvae, water fleas, dragonfly larvae, water boatmen and water beetles are just a few of the species which thrive in the mud on the floor of the canal. They periodically come to the surface for air.

It is easy to write off Lymm as a mere suburb of Warrington, especially by those who pass through it along the busy A56 road. Walk in along the Bridgewater Canal towpath, however, and Lymm is seen in its true context — yet another village which increased dramatically in importance because it was on the line of the Duke's canal.

The canal actually passes through just to the north of the village centre and from the moment of its opening Lymm became an important centre for the manufacture of fustian cloth. In the centre of the village is one of the finest sets of stocks to be found anywhere in Britain and overlooked by an equally impressive market cross which dates to the 17th century, although the well worn sandstone steps may be older. The cross was restored in 1897 to celebrate Queen Victoria's Diamond Jubilee. The steps have actually been cut out of a natural outcrop of rock.

Apart from having the advantage of the canal, one of Lymm's most attractive features is its dam, which was due not to any aquatic development but to the coming of the Turnpike Age. Stage coaches on their way from Manchester to Liverpool had to struggle up the steep Eagle Brow before making a sharp turn around the cross and up to the church and onwards into Cheshire. This route was so unreliable that a ravine, cut by the Bollin, was dammed in the 1850s thus creating a large lake, and a causeway road was constructed across it thus avoiding the steep climb up to the church. Around the same time the church itself was largely rebuilt, although its origins were more than likely back in Saxon times. There is a delightful legend concerning the church which tells of an old dame who came to pray each day and collected water from a spout. One day a hand emerged from the spout and snatched away the bucket. This emphasised that any water found in and around the church was to be regarded as Holy, which was obviously a throw back to the Catholic days prior to the Reformation.

The dam, and the church reflected in its waters, is one of the most sought after scenes for those who photograph Cheshire. The most attractive approach to the dam is via the wooded walk from the Dingle where pretty cottages are clustered along the banks of a stream.

Along the course of the Bridgewater Canal, which is crossed here by a hump backed bridge, there are many areas rich in natural history and Lymm Dam compares very favourably with any of them. In summer its fringes support a rich tapestry of vegetation on which depend insects of all shapes and sizes. These in turn are the food supplies used by birds, especially swallows, martins and swifts. Reed buntings, moorhen and coot all make use of the reed beds as feeding and breeding areas and in winter the variety of wildfowl is as varied as anywhere in Cheshire.

In August, Lymm has re-established its rushbearing festival, which takes us back to the time when churches had earth floors which were strewn with rushes brought from the hills on carts and with great ceremony. Villagers gave their time and their carts freely, but the Church responded by providing supplies of ale which allowed the ceremony to be one enjoyed with vigorous enthusiasm. The rushes kept the feet of the worshippers relatively dry and warm, and in medieval times it was rare to have pews for the general congregation. Such luxury was only provided for the gentry and the churchwardens, which is why early pews bore initials and family names. The hale and hearty stood up in the body of the church whilst the elderly and the sick were allowed to lean on the walls. This is the origin of the saying "the weakest go to the wall."

Lymm, as we have seen, became important because of the coming of the Bridgewater Canal but the nearby and prosperous, intially at least, village of Warburton was left in splendid isolation. Its turn was to come later with the building of the Manchester Ship Canal. Warburton had, until this time, been enfolded into the bank of the Mersey, but when the Ship Canal was constructed it took over the course of the river which was altered and Warburton then needed a toll bridge. At this point the Mersey and the Ship Canal are one and the same.

Warburton had a church before the Norman Conquest and derives its name from St. Werburgh who was the daughter of Wulfhere, the powerful King of Mercia. Other historians feel that this lady may have been a daughter of Alfred the Great. It is a delightful little church constructed around a timber frame but this is largely hidden by later claddings of half timbering and stone. On the north side of the church is a suspicious bulge which suggests that not all the planned additions and alterations to the church went smoothly. These imperfections, however, add to the interest of such grand old churches, as

Lymm Dam — haunt of angler, naturalist and picnickers and which has a footpath running around it.

does the rather incongruous square brick tower. The church itself may well be younger than the mighty yew tree found in the area, near which are a set of well preserved stocks.

The interior of St. Werburgh's is of interest mainly for the simplicity of its design, the whole structure being supported by three huge arches of timber, which were fastened together using dowels made from the antlers of red deer. The arches, in turn, rest upon six uprights which were also roughly hacked out of massive tree trunks. This initial dependence upon timber supports meant that it was not possible later on to add side aisles and thus the shape of the original church has had to be retained. This provides modern day visitors with a clear insight into medieval church construction.

A church of such simple design deserves equally simple furnishings and, again, Warburton does not disappoint. On the north side are a fascinating set of box pews bearing the inscription "William Drinkwater, the Keeper 1603". The present approach to Warburton would not be recognised by the Keeper but it has its attractions nevertheless. The village is still surrounded by farmland and has a metal toll bridge dating to 1863 when it crossed the Mersey. This was extended when the Ship Canal was built and although the Warburton Bridge does cope with a steady stream of light traffic it never seems to disturb the olde worlde tranquility of the village.

On its way to Grappenhall, the Bridgewater Canal skirts the ancient village of Thelwall now almost submerged by the complexities of the M6. The name means a pool by a plank bridge and derives from the Old English. The settlement merited an entry in the Anglo-Saxon chronicle but surprsingly not in the Domesday Book.

It is usually stated that Thelwall was founded in AD 923 by Edward the Elder, and many visitors arrive expecting to see items of great antiquity; they go away disappointed. This is a great pity but there is still plenty to see, including some delightful half-timbered cottages and there are firm written records relating to its connection with Edward the Elder.

After the Norman Conquest, Thelwall was in Ecclesiastical hands but by 1662 it was owned by the Pickering family, who later built a magnificent Georgian Hall. This hall, after use as a military office during the Second World War, was allowed to fall

Lymm Cross.

into disrepair and was then sadly demolished.

The church has a stained glass window, inserted in 1950, to celebrate the life of Sir Peter Rylands who worshipped here but made his fortune from his wire works based in Warrington. The area around Thelwall had long been an area of watermeadows which provided grazing for livestock in summer and during periods of winter flood were havens for waterfowl. Such areas were known as 'eyes' and Thelwall Eyes, beneath the M6 viaduct, is now managed as a nature reserve. Here, within the sound and sight of a busy motorway, rare birds are eagerly sought by ornithologists armed with the essential permits.

On the opposite side of the Bridgewater Canal, but within easy walking distance, is the village of Appleton Thorn which merits a substantial mention in any book devoted to the folklore and festivals of England. Have you, we wonder, ever baumed your thorn? Maybe you have not enjoyed this ceremony, but on the third Saturday in June this Cheshire village enjoys every minute of it.

Bauming the Appleton Thorn takes us back to the glorious days of Adam de Dutton, an Anglo-Norman knight, who returned safe and sound from his escapades during the 12th century crusades. He paused at Glastonbury in Somerset to give thanks for his safe return. He brought part of the Glastonbury Thorn, which is a hawthorn said to have sprouted from the staff thrust into the ground by Joseph of Arimathea, the uncle of Jesus, who sought refuge in England following the crucifixion. It flowers at Christmas and is therefore thought to be Holy. Adam de Dutton planted his offshoot in his own manor of Appleton and it was garlanded (baumed) every year until Victorian times when it lapsed. It has been revived since and a new tree was planted near the church in 1967. We need ceremonies such as 'Bauming the Thorn', to remind us that Olde England has its unique traditions which should be enjoyed and celebrated.

The British would travel miles to witness such an event in France, Italy and Spain so why should we neglect our own folklore. Why not take a June stroll along the canal and have a go at bauming your thorn while you are at it?

Grappenhall, which is directly on the line of the canal, is yet another pretty village which owes its period of 19th century prosperity to the coming of the Bridgewater, which almost slices it in two. The church, which is situated almost on the canal bank, has, according to most authorities, a claim to a place in the literary history of the world. Above the west window is a stone carving of a cat which has been given, by its sculptor, a most mischievous grin. It is thought that this may be the Cheshire Cat made famous in Lewis Carroll's *Alice in Wonderland* which is described fully in the next chapter.

Perhaps the cat's grin was due to its being able to watch folk in the stocks which are now situated close to the churchyard wall. Miscreants were pelted with rotten fruit by those intent upon avenging themselves on the local crooks. The cat, however, does seem to have had a place in local folklore for many centuries and there are wooden carvings of the animal in the furniture of several Cheshire churches.

Both Lymm and Grappenhall, although often now regarded as mere suburbs of Warrington, have retained most of the atmosphere they had when on the line of the busy Bridgewater Canal. These joys are there awaiting those who have the good sense to treat them as interesting places and seek out the many reminders of their past.

Although the river Mersey was then navigable up to Warrington, giving the town, then famous for the manufacture of sail cloth, access to the sea, the construction of the Bridgewater did bring substantial

Grappenhall Village photographed in 1920.

benefits. The proximity of the canal provided a trading link with the Lancashire coalfields and the potteries of the Midland counties via the Bridgewater and the Trent and Mersey Canals.

Warrington was settled prior to the coming of the Romans who soon fortified the area around Wilderspool, which was actually named later by the Saxons and translates as the place where "the wild deer drink". Here was a vital fording point of the Mersey before Warrington Bridge was built.

An important trading centre from the Middle Ages onwards, Warrington not only made sail cloth, but then came soap, brewing, wire making and scientific research all of which combined to make the town famous. There are now atomic research establishments close to the banks of the Bridgewater Canal between Grappenhall and Daresbury. These continue Warrington's scientific traditions which began in the 18th century when Joseph Priestley, the discoverer of oxygen and its properties, taught at Warrington Academy.

These atomic establishments, along with the rich and varied wildlife, add interest to the towpath walk towards Preston Brook, which is the subject of the next chapter.

CHAPTER EIGHT

Stockton Heath to Preston Brook via Daresbury

STOCKTON HEATH, another old village, is also now little more than a residential suburb of Warrington, but this is soon left behind as the Bridgewater Canal reaches Higher Walton. Between bridges 11 (Walton) and 12 (Walton Lea) the canal cuts its way through a wooded area, which results in some splendidly scenic reflections in the water.

Time should be spent here looking at Walton Hall, the present building dating to 1830, although substantial additions were made during the 1870s. This was once the home of Sir Gilbert Greenall, the founder of the brewing company of Greenall, Whitley which is still a major employer in the Warrington area. Among the attractions in the grounds of Walton Hall was once a small zoo, but of particular merit are the rose arbours and a magnificent conservatory.

The towpath passes through the attractive village of Moore, the quiet canal here contrasting sharply with the often busy road linking Runcorn with Warrington. Some of the canalside cottages hereabouts are among the prettiest to be found anywhere along the Bridgewater. Their beauty is often enhanced as colourful barges are reflected in the water. The speed restrictions imposed upon canal barges, and especially the potentially more powerful pleasure cruisers, reduce the ripples and wash which would destroy not only the reflections but more importantly erode the canal banks.

We have sometimes heard this stretch described as a walk through wonderland but perhaps this description owes more than a little to the next village along the canal. This is Daresbury, where one famous wonderland began because it is the birthplace of Lewis Carroll.

> *"I watch the drowsy night expire*
> *And fancy paints at my desire*
> *Her magic pictures in the fire.*
> *An island farm 'mid seas of corn*
> *Swayed by the wandering breath of morn*
> *The happy spot where I was born."*

These lines are taken from Lewis Carroll's poem

Daresbury Church and the baptism certificate of Charles Lutwidge Dodgson (alias Lewis Carroll).

"The Three Sunsets" and prove that the author had a real and lasting affection for his native county. The writer's real name was the Reverend Charles Lutwidge Dodgson who became a brilliant mathematician and wrote several learned books on this subject but is now best remembered as the author of *"Alice in Wonderland"* and *"Alice through the Looking Glass."*

Charles was born at the Old Parsonage, Newton-by-Daresbury on January 27th 1832. His father was the Reverend Charles Dodgson who later became the Arch-deacon of Richmond in Swaledale, Yorkshire. The maiden name of his mother, who was of German stock, was Lutwidge. His father was vicar of Daresbury from 1827 to 1843 and during this period he also ran a mission for the canal workers at the Preston Brook junction. Initially, the mission was situated on an old barge and young Charles must have been familiar with the bargees and the life of a working canal.

The old parsonage where Charles was born was about two miles from the parish church of All Saints, and had an associated Glebe Farm. In 1883, the house was destroyed by fire and only its old well remains. This is a great pity because it would have made a fine museum to celebrate the life of Lewis Carroll, and also the local countryside which so impressed him during his formative years.

Charles left Daresbury in 1843 and went to Rugby where he came under the invaluable influence of Dr Tait, who later became Archbishop of Canterbury. In 1850 the young scholar went up to Oxford and in 1854 graduated with a first in mathematics. He completed an equally impressive MA in 1857 and on December 22nd 1861 he was ordained as a Deacon. He never actually continued his theological studies to the stage where he could have been ordained priest. For the rest of his life Charles Lutwidge Dodgson lectured at Oxford and wrote fictional works under the name of Lewis Carroll. Never at ease with adults, Charles always found it easier to relate to children and wrote his books to amuse the daughters of his friends.

The search for one of England's greatest authors takes us to All Saints Church at Daresbury, which is itself under-rated, although there has been considerable rebuilding since the childhood days of Lewis Carroll. An ancient yew grows close to and shadows the south porch of the church. The squat square tower of sandstone is topped by a weather vane in the form of a fish, which has always been recognised as a symbol of Christianity. Sometimes the flagpole on the tower flies the flag of St. George. This adds to the atmosphere of the church because no author is more typical of the eccentric Englishman

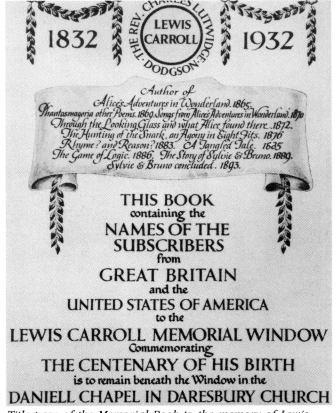

Title page of the Memorial Book to the memory of Lewis Carroll.

than Lewis Carroll. The views from the churchyard across the rolling countryside, however, can have changed but little since his obviously idyllic childhood.

There is written evidence that in 1159 Henry, the second Prior of Norton, which is described in the next chapter, provided funds for the construction of a church at Daresbury. This building is thought to have been of wood and plaster and with the exterior probably

The Lewis Carroll Memorial window.

The church at Daresbury remained under the control of Norton Priory throughout the Middle Ages, but following Henry VIII's Reformation all monastic property was either sold or redistributed. All Saints was given into the hands of Christ Church, Oxford and this situation lasted until the late 19th century. The College had the right to collect the tithes from Daresbury Parish which then included Preston o'th Hill, Newton-by-Daresbury, Moore, Hatton, Keckwick and Higher and Lower Walton.

Just prior to the Reformation of the 1550s the wooden church at Daresbury was replaced by a stone structure and by the 19th century this building was showing signs of wear and tear.

A "complete restoration" of the church and tower was funded by Sir Gilbert Greenall, baronet and brewer of Walton Hall. He did this "in remembrance of a faithful domestic Esther Lurtin who bequeathed to her master the earnings of long service." It is also recorded that the main body of the church was "destroyed" in 1870 but had been rebuilt by 1872. This Victorian building was designed in the old Gothic style in a surprisingly good effort to copy the great parish churches and spectacular cathedrals of the Middle Ages. It did, however, alter the church which would have been so well known to Lewis Carroll.

Some of the furnishings of All Saints are obviously much older than the date of this rebuilding and the church registers date back to 1600, when it seems as if a conscious effort was made to put the secretarial affairs of the church in order. Here also is the baptismal certificate relating to Charles Lutwidge Dodgson which is dated July 11th, 1832.

The contents of the church may well have influenced the future writer, and of particular interest

painted which accounted for its alternative name of "The White Church of Cheshire". On the south side of the tower the number 1110 has been carved but Beaumont, an early 20th century local historian, suggests that this date should actually be 1550. During an extensive 17th century restoration, weathering led to an error. The workman misread the original fives for ones, and thus inscribed his mistake in stone.

in this context is an illustrated rhyme giving an amusing warning to the bell ringers. Daresbury has an impressive ring of eight bells, four of which were cast by Randal of Gloucester in 1725. The rhyme which was put in place in 1730, reads:-

> **D**are *not to come into this Sacred Place*
> **A**ll *you good Ringers, but in awful Grace*
> **R**ing *not with Hatt, nor Spurs nor Insolence*
> **E**ach *one that does, for every such offence*
> **S**hall *forfeit Hatt or Spurs or Twelve Pence*
> **B**ut *who disturbs a Peal the same Offender*
> **U**nto *the Box his Sixpence shall down Tender*
> **R**ules *such no doubt in every Church are used*
> **Y**ou *and your Bells that may not be abused.*

The initial letters of each word in the rhyme form the word DARESBURY, a formation known as an acrostic. Most experts on the writings of Lewis Carroll think that from his early life he may have been fascinated by, and become an expert on, the construction of acrostics. He produced many of these, which greatly pleased the children of his friends.

It is entirely appropriate that Lewis Carroll should have his own magnificent memorial within the church and this is in the form of a magnificent stained glass window. It is situated at the east end of the Daniell chapel. The window was designed by Geoffrey Webb and was paid for by a memorial fund subscribed to by "Alice fans" from all over the world. It was dedicated on June 30th 1934 by the Bishop of Warrington.

The window is a balanced combination of the religious and the secular and thus perfectly appropriate for a literary man with an ecclesiastical background. The influence of mathematics on the life of Dodgson is not forgotten either. The top of the window shows a scene from the nativity with all the obvious characters present, including Joseph, Mary and the infant Jesus in His cradle. Beneath this the words from Lewis Carroll's poem "Christmas Greetings" have been inscribed:

> *"We have heard the children say*
> *Gentle children whom we love*
> *Long Ago on Christmas Day*
> *Came a message from above."*

A study of the left hand side of the Nativity reveals Carroll himself wearing a surplice and hood and close to him is Alice. The original young lady is said to have been Alice Liddell the daughter of the Dean of Christ Church, Oxford. Christ Church, as we have already seen, controlled the parish of Daresbury following the Reformation.

The religious theme of the window is sandwiched between a celebration of the author and his books. At the apex of the window is the Wheatsheaf, which is the symbol of the County of Cheshire where he was born, and beneath are two heraldic shields. One is of Rugby school the other of Christ's Church, Oxford which between them trained the scholar and the man. In this area of the window there are also two small lights, one showing a pair of compasses and the other a lamp of learning, together celebrating the life of one of the more able mathematicians of Victorian England.

The portion of the window so far described tends to be overlooked by most visitors, whose eyes are understandably drawn to the bottom section which depicts the well loved illustrations by Sir John Tenniel from the Alice books. Here are The White Rabbit,

Bill the Lizard, the Dodo, Caterpillar, Fish-Footman, the Mad Hatter, the Dormouse sitting in the tea-pot, the March Hare, the Duchess, the Gryphon, the Mock Turtle, the Knave of Hearts, the Queen of Hearts and of course the Cheshire Cat. The dedication on the window reads "In memory of Charles Lutwidge Dodgson (Lewis Carroll) author of Alice in Wonderland". He died at Guildford on January 14th 1898.

Apart from the window itself the Daniell chapel has many features of interest to devotees of Lewis Carroll. There is, for example, an oak desk containing an album listing the names of all who subscribed to the window fund. The desk was made from timber taken from the 16th century church during the rebuilding of 1872. Some of the subscribers were Americans which underlines how many of its citizens love their *Alice in Wonderland*. When the original manuscript of Alice came up for sale in 1929 it was bought by the American book collector Dr. A.S.W. Rosenback for the then enormous sum of £15,400.

Visitors should also seek out a cupboard on which can be seen illustrations of the original Parsonage House before it burned down and also the interior of the old church as the young Dodgson would have known it.

There is no doubt that, but for the life of Lewis Carroll, Daresbury church would be much less visited, although there are many other points of interest. In the Daniell chapel for example there is some fine panelling below the Carroll window and within this is a painting showing Christ breaking bread. This picture was given by the Rylands family of Warrington. The chapel also has a fine collection of memorials to the Chadwick family of Daresbury

Hall and whose vault was situated below the chapel in the old church. This was once named after this family but in recent years it has been renamed after the Daniells who, in fact, had a much more ancient connection with Daresbury.

In the chancel there are also a number of fine memorial tablets and plaques of which by far the best is dedicated to Sarah Byrom. This was fashioned by the 19th century English sculptor John Gibson but who worked out of Rome and was well thought of in Italy. The work bears an inscription in the lower left hand corner which reads "Gibson Fecit Roma". The theme of Sarah Byrom's memorial was a familiar one of the period and illustrates a young woman dying in childbirth and being guided gently towards heaven by an angel. Her distraught young husband is seen left grieving at her feet.

Also on view are two items of ornately carved furniture. The oak pulpit dates from 1625 and is one of the best examples in Cheshire. Its Jacobean woodcarving depicts not only the predictable angels but also a number of grotesque figures. This, and also the carved chancel screen, belonged to the old church. Prior to the Reformation, the rood screen was positioned in the chancel to conceal the choir and the high altar from the congregation. Medieval religion was magnificently full of pomp and ceremony but was always very élitist. The preparation for the mass was very much a secret ceremony. When the church was rebuilt the screen was sensibly, although unusually, retained but it could not be allowed to be so dominant as it had been in the past. It was therefore cut down to form a low partition between the nave and the chancel at the entrance to the choir but some sections were also incorporated into the panelling behind the altar. It is worth seeking out some of these carvings, especially one section showing a "Green Man" which takes us back to the ancient pagan religion based on the natural world and which, in Saxon times, was replaced by Christianity.

Early craftsmen paid homage to their new religion, but occasionally carved reminders of the old pagan figures, perhaps to hedge their bets just in case the Christians were in error! Even at Norton Priory, described in the next chapter, we will find that the pagans still refused to be totally dominated by Christian doctrine.

CHAPTER NINE

Preston Brook to Runcorn
via Norton Priory

THIS CHAPTER concludes our journey along the Bridgewater Canal. At its junction with the Trent and Mersey canal at Preston Brook the main line comes to an end. The Duke of Bridgewater, however, had his financially ambitious eyes on the Mersey. Any canal with a direct link to the sea must have been irresistible to industrialists with their sights set firmly on foreign exports.

As we have also mentioned several times in the course of our journey along the Bridgewater it is almost always under-rated by walkers and this is particularly the case with regard to the section leading from Preston Brook to Runcorn. Here the canal was once linked, via locks, to the Mersey estuary and later to the Manchester Ship Canal. Whilst the Duke was supervising this extension he built himself a three storeyed Georgian-style residence in Runcorn, which still stands but is not open to the public. There are several sites along the canal which would appear to be ideal for the setting up of a Bridgewater Museum. This mansion is another.

Norton Priory undercroft, built c.1200.

A most attractive walk follows the towpath from the village of Moore to Runcorn, both places are best reached from the car park of Norton Priory. This is an historical Phoenix, having risen in recent years from the ashes of neglect. This splendid ruin is signed from Junction 11 off the M56. It is well worth paying the modest entry fee, which includes the right to follow a meandering but well marked footpath through the magnificently colourful gardens down to the bank of the Bridgewater Canal. This bank is, however, not on the main towpath but merely a pleasant extention of the Norton Priory walk. The priory has a museum, shop, cafe and a picnic site.

Norton Priory was the home of an influential group of Augustinians established in the area in 1115 when they were given land by the Baron of Halton. In 1134 the monks moved from their first home to the present site at Norton which was then even closer to the wide estuary of the Mersey than it is today. Between the priory and the Mersey we now have the Bridgewater Canal and the soaring embankments of the Manchester Ship Canal. In the 12th century this area was sand, mud and salt marsh, a dream for wildlife but a nightmare for unwary travellers.

On display in the priory is a huge and splendidly spectacular sandstone statue of St. Christopher the Patron Saint of travellers. This statue, which dates to 1391, must have been a popular shrine for guests of the priory in need of a quick prayer to see them safely over the Mersey in the days before bridges, reliable ferry boats and tunnels.

Norton was an important monastic house, although never listed among the larger houses. At its peak the priory had been raised to the status of an abbey and there were twenty four Augustinians in residence under the control of an Abbot. The job of the brethren was to look after the spiritual side of the house with their bodily needs mainly catered for by servants. Food was produced from the numerous monastic farms which were spread far and wide throughout the country, including local estates but with some as far distant as Lincolnshire, Nottinghamhire and Oxfordshire. A medieval abbey evolved from a simple gathering of religious men into a huge company run along similar lines to big businesses today. Salesmen and accountants were very much part of a monastic institution.

The Augustinians were known as the Black Canons because they wore an outer cape of black wool over the top of a white linen surplice. They wore leather boots and as they farmed their own sheep and cattle they were self sufficient in apparel as well as food. The Augustinians were allowed to eat well and enjoyed two substantial meals during each day. They ate beef, lamb or pork and the monastic gardens cultivated peas, beans and other vegetables. They baked bread, drank their own ale and beer and ate plenty of fruit, especially apples and pears from their own orchards. The unpolluted Mersey could always be guaranteed to provide a surfeit of fish and there were also substantial salt deposits around the estuary. The brothers' main occupation, however, was centred around the services in their church on which the bulk of their income was spent. They were prepared to offer prayers for the souls of those who were generous to the abbey. This required some organisational skills as the "prayer load" was already heavy.

The monastic routine evolved to fit in to the natural day, only using candles or rush lighting when absolutely necessary. At 2.30am the brethren would rise from their dorter and wind their way in procession down stone stairs to the church. Each probably carried a flickering candle and the smell of the hot wax would fill the nostrils and the acrid fumes cause the eyes to smart. After a period of prayer and psalm chanting, the first service of the day was the Nocturn was quickly followed by Matins, during which dawn was quite likely to break and throw its cold light onto the kneeling brothers.

If dawn came late, as it does during the winter months, the monks waited, doubtless shivering with cold, for first light. When this came it was greeted by a service called Prime after which they were allowed to sit in or walk around the cloisters or read until 8am, by which time they must have been pretty hungry. Strict monastic life, however, meant getting used to hunger, but as we have seen the Norton brethren did feed rather well. The Cistercian order was rather more frugal.

Soon this short period of relaxation was over and after a quick wash and brush up in the lavatorium, which in those days meant a splash of freezing water from stone basins set into the wall of the toilet block (reredorter), it was back to the church. Two services were held at this time which were called Terce and Morrow Mass. There tended to be one monastic service for each hour in the day, and skilled monks prepared illustrated manuscripts each of which was called a Book of Hours. Some monasteries, such as Lindisfarne and Jarrow, became famous for their books of hours, but all establishments had skilled illuminators. Most of these were destroyed at the time of the Reformation.

Morrow Mass was followed by a formal meeting

The Georgian House around Norton Priory. Photographed in 1920 prior to its sad demolition.

in the chapter house which was named because at this time a chapter from the gospels was read. This was also the time when the abbot issued his orders to his brothers and after the main business of the day had been outlined there was a period which could be devoted to private study. At midday, however, prayer again took over and three services were held. These were Sext, High Mass which was the main service of the day, and None.

Then, at last, it was time for a period of serious eating and the brothers trooped eagerly into the Frater or dining room. Most abbeys were famous both for their food and for their hospitality to visitors, who used them as we use hotels, with the enviable exception that board and lodging up to a maximum of three days was provided free. The poor, however, were always sure of a generous hand out.

Reflections on the Bridgewater Canal near to Norton Priory.

After the meal the afternoon in the life of a monk has been described as free, although this is a rather loose term. They were expected either to engage in physical labour about the abbey or alternatively, devote themselves to study. Looking at the organisation of Norton Priory today, it is nice to think that a monk may have strolled through the gardens thinking about the beauties of nature, set among the flowers and have a snooze lulled by the buzzing of the bees and the gentle trill of bird song.

All too soon on days like this five o'clock arrived and it was back into church for the next service, which was called Vespers. Then, after a short break for another but much lighter meal there was a Bible reading followed by the Compline service which brought the day to an end. Brethren were usually in their dormitories by 7pm to build up strength for another day of prayer.

The main benefactors of these hard working monks were initially the Barons of Halton but the Dutton family were also generous. The latter had extensive lands at Sutton and at Warburton and they gave land, the income from churches in their manors, tithes and even direct gifts of money. The Duttons' generosity allowed Norton Priory to employ the best craftsmen and use the best materials. The best sandstone rock came from Windmill Hill about a mile from Norton and this kept costs down to a minimum. The master mason was almost certainly Hugh de Cathewick who was brought from his home at Cathwick near Beverley in Yorkshire.

The Duttons were rewarded for their generosity by having prayers said to ensure that their dead rested in peace and with regular prayers chanted for the good of their souls. Scattered around the ruins of the priory church area the sandstone coffins of the Dutton family can still be seen and some of the skeletons removed from these have been subjected to careful forensic examinations.

It seems that the 14th and 15th century Duttons were about the same average height as the present day population, although perhaps just a fraction shorter. Their diet was sugar free in those days and their teeth seem to have been significantly more healthy than is the case with many people of today. Some use was made of honey, for which many abbeys were famous, but it was not used in sufficient quantity to cause dental problems. It does seem, however, that arthritic problems were more frequent in those days. People probably worked harder and travel was tougher whilst they were housed in much damper, colder conditions than we have to endure in days of easy transport, mechanised agricultural and industrial machinery and central heating.

The abbey complex at Norton was grouped around a square cloister garden. A covered passage called the cloister walk had a garden on each side and through this the rest of the abbey buildings could be reached. The church, typically designed in the shape of a cross, was to the north whilst the south side was occupied by the chapter house. This was the focal point from which the abbot could communicate with his brethren and the rules of St. Augustine could be explained to novice monks and emphasised to the erring souls who ought to have known better.

Close to the chapter house was the warming room which was the only area in the monastery where there was a fire specifically ignited to give the

The village of Moore on the Bridgewater Canal.

brethren comfort. Above the warming room the dormitory was very sensibly situated to take advantage of the rising hot air and to the south of the warming room there was the reredorter or toilet block. To the south of the cloister were the refectory and kitchens. On the western side of the abbey was the undercroft or storerooms and above these the abbot had his personal suite of rooms.

When the abbey was dissolved on the orders of Henry VIII in 1536 most of the buildings were stripped of valuable timber and especially of its roofing lead. Only the undercroft survived almost intact and which dates to around 1200. It is composed of three spacious bays to the south, each with splendid ribbed vaulting and at the northern end are four bays, the architecture of which are somewhat obscured by brick wine bins which were built during the 18th century.

At the northern end a passage dating to around

1190 still exists which once provided a connection between the store rooms and the parlour. The monks had spent more time and expense on this area than on the store rooms which were not likely to be seen by many visitors. Abbeys from about 1400 onwards felt it necessary to impress visitors who were important business contacts and prepared meeting rooms, much as our companies spend revenue on their board rooms.

The abbot's lodgings above the undercroft, after years of 'neglect, have now been converted into a viewing area and a taped commentary helps visitors to identify the foundations of the long ruined church, refectory and the ingenious drainage system which was particularly intricate around the reredorter, the kitchens and the infirmary.

After 1536 the buildings were apparently left open to the weather but in 1545 Norton Priory and its associated estates were sold to Sir Richard Brooke who built a typical Tudor manor house using stone from the abbey. Apparently, Sir Richard paid £1512 1s 9d for Norton and his house was planned around the outer courtyard. He retained the gatehouse, brewhouse, abattoir, dairy, barn and stables. He chose the abbot's personal suite and the west range as the central features of his new house.

We have to remember that during the later Tudor period all Catholic institutions were feared and hated and this explains why the Brookes chose to neglect the church and the cloisters, using these areas as rubbish dumps and during later excavations a battered leather shoe of the period was unearthed from what had been the family tip.

The Brooke family seem to have managed the former monastic estates rather well and the profits,

A modern sculpture in the gardens of Norton Priory.

added to those of their original estates at Leighton near Crewe, enabled them to enjoy the privileged life style of country gentlefolk.

Their Tudor house proved to be a solid base until 1750 when it was beginning to need extensive repairs and it was decided to demolish it and construct a typical early Georgian Mansion. Surprisingly, neither the precise date of completion nor the architect are known, but we must be grateful that the priory undercroft was incorporated into the new building and was then used for its original function of storage. In the late 18th century James Wyatt was employed to plan some modifications. In 1868, the undercroft was adapted, although it was not substantially damaged, in order to produce a rather splendid entrance hall and a porch was dovetailed onto the west side of the Georgian House. A splendid Romanesque doorway was also incorporated into the entrance complex and a rather well made Victorian replica was added to the opposite side and successfully achieved architectural balance.

The Brooke family, in the late 18th century, entered upon a long period of acrimonious dispute with the Duke of Bridgewater who wished to cut his canal through the family lands. This was yet another example of the canal construction generating controversies which were later repeated throughout Britain during the Railway Age of Victorian times, and is still a bone of contention when modern roads and motorways are planned.

By the 1920s the Brooke family had left the estate and following a period of neglect their Georgian mansion crumbled away and was eventually demolished. The site of this important old priory became overgrown. Then, thankfully, came the Norton Priory Trust who now maintain the estate which is slowly but surely being returned to its medieval magnificence, but the wonderful walled garden, so beloved by the Brooke family, has now been splendidly replanted.

Modern sculptors have been commissioned to produce statues which have been sensitively sited among the streams and woodlands which are linked by well signed footpaths. The statues include that of a very contented monk who looks out over the herb garden, a life sized Madonna depicted in her black Augustinian habit, stands at the junction of a woodland path, and among the limpid depths of a small pond the form of Conventia, the Celtic goddess of streams and wells, peeps out from among the weeds. Another sculpture called Planthead has been sited among the rhododendrons, which are a joy especially in May and June. Spring is celebrated at Norton first by hosts of daffodils which would have even impressed the Wordsworths and later by aromatic waves of bluebells. The monks often 'farmed' bluebells, collecting the bulbs and boiling them up in water to produce an apparently very efficient glue which they used to bind paper together to produce books. The Old English word for the bark of a tree was 'bok' which meant that leaves from trees could be written on and stuck with glue between strips of boks. The terminology has changed little today. We still turn over a new leaf!

The Norton Priory Trust really have done a splendid job not only within the priory gardens but also with the monastic artefacts and the buildings themselves. Here can be found a bell and two summerhouses. In 1977 a replica was made of a 13th century bell cast for the priory. Enough of the original mould was found on site to enable the new bell to be cast.

Restoration has also been carried out on the late 18th century summerhouse said to have been designed by James Wyatt during the period that he was working on the Georgian mansion. The floor of the summerhouse was relaid in 1978 using tiles made

Reflections on the Bridgewater Canal near Norton.

from local clay but fired in an experimental kiln of medieval design. The tile designs were copied from those excavated from the nave of the Priory church. It is known that the church itself and the chapter house were re-tiled in the 15th century. It was usual for the itinerant workers to make their tiles on site and their kiln was excavated in 1972. A stoking area was found with access points to two firing chambers and the tiles were baked in ovens constructed above these. The oven temperature would have reached more than 1000°C. The clay was cut whilst still wet and patterns were impressed using templates drawn by skilled artists. They had available more than 20 patterns depicting flowers and animals, including lions.

The larger of the two summerhouses in the gardens was built in 1829 in the classical temple style and situated close to the replica of the medieval bell. The Brooke family intended to use the building as an indoor picnic area and Mary Brooke's journal refers to the woodland temple with great affection. They were all fond of their home and it is no wonder that they felt threatened by the Duke of Bridgewater's canal, which was a potential threat to their rural tranquility and a magnet to their servants wanting to earn more money.

For the walk from the priory to the canal itself, along its towpath, it is best to choose a bright day and follow the obvious path via the playing fields to the right of the Priory gates and car park. The reflections of the trees and bridges in the waters of the canal can be spectacular. Inland, the towpath leads towards the villages of Moore and Daresbury.

The walk towards Runcorn and the Mersey estuary passes the town park which is usually full of birds, many of which breed in the reeds and hopeful fishermen always seem to be present and who try their luck both here and along the canal itself. Fiddlers Ferry power station forms a surprisingly attractive backdrop to the Bridgewater as it continues towards Old Runcorn.

These days the canal terminates suddenly at the double arched Waterloo Bridge which has ornate iron railings. The set of ten locks, once arranged in a double staircase, have either vanished altogether or at best are derelict. One set was abandoned in 1949, the second in 1966. In view of the recent developments in the tourist industry the loss of contact with the Ship Canal, the Mersey and with Runcorn Docks cannot be over estimated. From Runcorn Docks the short Runcorn and Weston Canal led to Weston Point and from this area there was easy access to the river Weaver. The remarkable Anderton lift connected the Weaver with the Trent and Mersey Canal. This lift is being repaired at considerable expense. Would it, we wonder, ever be possible to rebuild the Runcorn locks?

Runcorn these days is considered merely as a modern industrial town, earning its living largely from the chemical industry. Two points are, however, missed. Firstly, Runcorn has a fascinating early history and secondly, its industrial development came purely because of the Bridgewater Canal, which was initially locked down into the Mersey estuary and thus at the point of entry to the sea.

There had been an important crossing of the Mersey at Runcorn probably in prehistoric times which was certainly well used by the Romans. The Saxons were also aware of the strategic importance of this crossing and built Halton Castle with the express purpose of defending it. They called the settlement around the estuary Runcofan.

Runcorn stands upon the Cheshire Bank with Widnes across the Mersey on the Lancashire side. Some historians have suggested that Runcorn as a town may have been established by Aethelfleda the daughter of King Alfred in AD 915.

The name Mersey simply means "the boundary river" and at this point the water is squeezed into a narrow gap before widening out again into the estuary between New Brighton and Liverpool. For centuries a row-boat ferry operated between Widnes and Runcorn. This was made famous in one of Stanley Holloway's monologues.

> *"On the banks of the Mersey, over on Cheshire side*
> *Lies Runcorn that's best known to fame*
> *By Transporter Bridge as tak's folks over its stream*
> *Or else brings 'em back across same.*
>
> *In the days afore Transporter Bridge were put up*
> *A ferry boat lay in the slip*
> *And old Ted the boatman would row folks across*
> *At per tuppence per person per trip."*

These days the Mersey is spanned between Runcorn and Widnes by an impressive steel arched road bridge which is 330 metres (1,082 feet) wide. This was completed in 1961 and was then the third largest such construction in the world. It replaced the even more famous early twentieth century transporter bridge which consisted of moving carriages which could be loaded with vehicles and carried over the river by steel cables.

Another feature of the Runcorn Gap is the railway bridge and viaduct built in 1869. This has a footpath running parallel to the railway line and it was this

which brought Stanley Holloway's ferry to an end. It is a great pity that the Transporter Bridge was demolished to make room for the present bridge. What a wonderful tourist attraction it could have become.

Whether the river was crossed by ferry or by bridge, this area was of vital importance both for commerce and in times of war. There was considerable activity in this area during the Civil War, at the conclusion of which Cromwell had Halton Castle demolished because it controlled the river crossing.

Just to the west of Fiddlers Ferry is an interesting hump still often referred to by the locals as "Cromwells Bank" which must have offered commanding views across the Mersey gap and perhaps also provided intelligence concerning troop movements as far away as Warrington Bridge. Surely the astute generals of the Civil War must have made use of Halton Castle, dominating a knoll on the Cheshire bank and which also provided panoramic views all the way upstream to Warrington as well as down the Mersey to the estuary.

The once magnificent old castle and the attractive church still stand together on a red sandstone bluff, defying wind and weather and dominating the scene below. Barges on the Bridgewater and later ocean going vessels on the Ship Canal were, and still are, easily seen from this vantage point.

Halton Castle had its origins way back in Saxon times when it was probably made of wood (the motte) and which was surrounded by a courtyard and a wall of earth and timber (the bailey). A more powerful stone structure was erected soon after the conquest by the Norman Barons of Halton from which they controlled the initially unruly Saxons. Maybe the locals here lacked the diplomacy of the Traffords described in an earlier chapter and did not compromise with the invaders. William FitzNigel, the second Norman Baron of Halton, established an Augustinian monastery at Runcorn in 1115 but in 1134, as we have seen the monks moved to Norton.

Things hereabouts were still far from peaceful when Langland wrote his narrative poem "Piers Plowman" in the 14th century. In the quaint Chaucerian style of the period he wrote:

"Thoro the pass of Haltoun
People might passe whith owte peril of robbyrye".

During its "working" life the castle fulfilled many rôles. Halton was, for example, one of the numerous residences to come into the possession of John of Gaunt who used it mainly as a hunting lodge. When his son Bolingbroke became King Edward I (1272-1307) Halton was absorbed into the lands of the Duchy of Lancaster and by 1579 it was being used as a prison for recusants. These were Catholics who refused to accept first Henry VIII and then Elizabeth I as Head of the English Church and held fast to their alliegance to the Pope. What dreadful scenes of torment must have been enacted within these now ruined walls. Between Henry and Elizabeth, England was ruled by Mary Tudor (1553-1558) who was a fanatical Catholic. During her reign the place of the recusants at Halton was taken by equally bigoted Protestant prisoners, many of whom were executed for their faith. They had their revenge when the Protestant Elizabeth succeeded Catholic Mary.

By virtue of its position and the stoutness of its walls, Halton must have been one of the most secure castles in England until the advent of artillery. It was Sir William Brereton's "field pieces" which battered the Royalist garrison almost into submission during 1643, but the defenders were relieved by the timely arrival of Prince Rupert. Later in the year the Prince was called away to fight more urgent battles. Brereton, aware of his second chance, returned and this time was able to complete his task. At the end of the war in the late 1640s the castle was "slighted". This was a term used by Cromwell's parliament to describe the knocking down of the defences of a castle so that it could never again be used as a fortress. The ruin was then sold to Henry Brooke but in 1660, when Charles II was restored to the throne, the castle ruin reverted once more to the Crown.

Halton was initially the most important settlement because of its castle and it obviously controlled the docks at Runcorn set in a creek on the Mersey. Runcorn was Halton's port and the two were mutually dependent upon each other.

The area around Runcorn and Widnes must have been idyllic in medieval times and even during the 17th and early 18th centuries a serious and almost successful attempt was made to establish the area as a health resort which was to be named Montpelier.

With the coming of the chemical industry based upon salt and coal which began in the late 18th century, all prospects of a health resort vanished at a stroke. The development of the chemical industry is graphically explained in a museum at Halton set up specifically for the purpose.

Initially, the Sankey Canal was important to the development of Runcorn and especially Widnes but the real heyday of the former only came as a direct result of the construction of the Bridgewater Canal. As the Sankey Canal actually pre-dates the Bridgewater a brief mention should be made of it here, if only

Widnes–Runcorn bridge which crosses the Mersey and overlooks both the Manchester Ship Canal and the Bridgewater.

to explain why the latter is considered to be the first canal in England.

The Sankey Brook, also known as the St Helens Canal, ran for eight miles, had ten locks including an impressive two rise staircase and linked St Helens with the Mersey. Since it was completed in 1757, two years before work started on the Bridgewater, why is the Sankey Brook not regarded as England's

first canal? The answer depends upon how one defines a canal. The Sankey Brook, as its name implies, followed the line of an already existing watercourse, whereas the Bridgewater was entirely independent of any existing river system and even, as we have seen, obtained its water directly from the run off from the Worsley mines.

What the Sankey Brook did was to allow a glass

industry to dominate the industrial life of St Helens, which it still does in the form of the world famous Pilkington Company. The history of glassmaking is explained in the impressive Glass Museum set up and maintained by the Company.

Although the Sankey Canal gave a boost to Widnes and Runcorn it was the Bridgewater which provided the latter's real launching pad. Between 1801 and 1847 the population of Runcorn increased fourfold and, for a while, it became a port quite independent of Liverpool and actually a serious rival to it. For a short time, Liverpool was dependent upon Runcorn as red sandstone quarried in this area was shipped down the Mersey for use in the construction of Liverpool's expanding docks and municipal buildings.

Runcorn's demise was due not to Liverpool but to Manchester as the completion of the Ship Canal created a massive inland port which operated at full swing from the day of its opening. This shifted the focus from Runcorn and the Bridgewater directly to Manchester via the Ship Canal. The city soon eclipsed the port of Runcorn. Its shipbuilding yards were isolated from deep water by the high walls of the Ship Canal and the workmen had to switch their skills to the "Sprinch" yards. Sprinch was a local term which referred to the construction of canal barges rather than larger sea going craft. The Old Quay on the Mersey which was linked to the Bridgewater Canal by a locking system fell into disuse. The loss of this outlet strangled some of the trade on the Bridgewater, although it continued to have an important line into the Potteries via the Trent and Mersey from Preston Brook. Despite this the loss of its sea arm at Runcorn was a disaster from which it could never fully recover.

The Bridgewater from the opening of the Ship Canal onwards was on a downward economic slope. It is only recently that tourism has breathed new life into the Duke's canal and allowed those who love it to look to the future with some optimism.

In 1995 we were asked to write and present documentary programmes for Greater Manchester Radio and BBC Radio Merseyside. The subjects were the Bridgewater and the Manchester Ship Canals. We were helped a great deal by the Ship Canal Company and it was whilst studying their archives that we were able to explore what is left of the link between the Bridgewater and the Manchester Ship Canal.

We found Waterloo Bridge near Runcorn Old Town which is the last span of the Bridgewater, now hemmed in by a complex ring road close to the Widnes Runcorn Bridge. We examined the plans of the link between the canals and the Mersey whilst sitting in the comfort of the Port Director's office. From the offices we followed a footpath and found the splendid Georgian house built by the Duke as he supervised the building of the Mersey link. The structure is in splendid repair and amid a tangle of old boats, decaying warehouses and vegetation including willowherb and bramble we found the old lock gates. This we regard as the tomb of the Bridgewater and these locks once fed water firstly into the Mersey and later into the Ship Canal.

This may be the tomb of the Bridgewater Canal but all might not be lost. Once it is realised that there is money in tourism there might yet be a link into the Bridgewater Canal. The present authors cannot wait for this to happen but whether it comes sooner or later the Bridgewater Canal will continue to enthrall us as much in the future as it ever has in the past.

CHAPTER TEN

The Bridgewater's Recent History

& Relations with the Manchester Ship Canal

WHENEVER THE Canal Age or the Railway Age which followed it are mentioned, the impression is often given that the owners had what amounted to a licence to print money. This was, in fact, far from the case as both were initially very high risk enterprises.

The Duke of Bridgewater almost bankrupted himself until his canal, and those which evolved because of it, began to run at a profit. He was an elderly man before he was free from mortgages and was able to afford extravagances such as the enlargement of his art collection. The Duke's critics have suggested that Francis Egerton was a buffoon who had not benefited from his education and who collected art but knew nothing about it. This condemns the experts as much as it does the Duke himself. The old man never enthused about anything but he would hardly have surrounded himself with objects which did not interest him. After years of poverty he began to indulge himself a little. By this time he had become a somewhat crusty old bachelor but very aware of the need to safeguard his assets. This became very apparent immediately following his death in 1803 when his will was found to be something of a legal minefield.

He left his collieries and beloved canal to be run by a trust of three people which was to apply for "as long as the lives of all the Peers of the House of Lords and their sons who were living at the time of the Duke's death and for a further 21 years as allowed by law." This stipulation did, in fact, operate for far longer than even the old Duke may have intended and it did not cease to function until 1903. The terms of the will did not prevent the owners of the mines and canal from making decisions, but there can be no doubt that their hands were legally tied and Francis thus influenced events long after his death.

The main beneficiary of the will was Lord Francis Leveson Gower who eventually (in 1837) came to live at Worsley, and according to the dictates of the will changed his name to Lord Francis Egerton. As we have seen earlier in this book, this man came to be greatly respected in and around Worsley and his philanthropy resulted in him being created the Earl of Ellesmere in 1846.

As the Duke of Bridgewater was developing his canal he did not always have an easy passage and earlier chapters have briefly described his legal battles with the owners of Trafford Park, Dunham Massey and Norton Priory who resisted, with varying degrees of success, any intrusion or interference to their, hitherto, peaceful estates.

The Duke's successors found that the boot was well and truly on the other foot and from 1825 onwards they themselves were fighting a rearguard action against the railways, whose noise, steam and smoke destroyed at a stroke the relative tranquility of the Canal Age. The Bridgewater Trustees fought tooth and nail against the setting up of the Manchester to Liverpool railway which was first suggested as early as 1825.

There was usually only one way to appease businessmen and that was to present them with financial incentives. A Bridgewater "life tenant" was offered 1,000 free shares in the Railway Company and the Canal Company was also given the right to appoint three directors to the Railway Company. The life tenants thus safeguarded their interest in the waterway but, even so, their relationship with the railway was never easy. The only real beneficiaries were probably those in the legal profession because more than 150 Parliamentary Bills had to be drawn up to achieve a balance between the canal and the railway companies' interests. A railway link between Worsley and Eccles, for example, did not come until 1861. Perhaps to allay the fears of their potential rivals, the railway directors travelled to witness the cutting of the first sod on the ground to

Francis Egerton III, Duke of Bridgewater 1736–1803.

be occupied by Worsley railway station in the comfort of a canal barge!

Running parallel with their dealings regarding the railways, the Bridgewater Trustees also spent time, effort and considerable sums of money during the first half of the 19th century improving the canal network. In 1838, for example, great expense was accepted in order to ease the problems caused by floodwaters from the river Medlock at the Castlefield Terminus in Manchester. Floodgates were constructed and a sophisticated overflow system evolved.

The Irwell itself also caused problems from time to time and these were solved at the same time by the construction of the Hulme Locks as well as canalising part of the river itself. This brought the Bridgewater Canal Company into even closer competition with the Mersey and Irwell Navigation Company, a problem which was only solved by purchasing the latter for £550,000. This enormous outlay of capital is an indication of how important to commerce the Bridgewater Canal was at that time.

By 1851 the Bridgewater was still a force to be reckoned with, and Lord Ellesmere's status was high enough to be worthy of a visit by Queen Victoria and even to merit a substantial entry in the monarch's diary. The Royal party arrived at Patricroft railway station and Victoria later wrote:

"We walked through a covered and prettily ornamented corridor to the boat which was waiting for us on the canal. It was a very elegant barge, to which a rope was fastened, drawn by four horses. Ourselves, the ladies, Lady Brackley and her little boy, the Old Duke and Capt Egerton came into it with us. Half was entirely covered in; the other half had an awning over it. The boat glided along in a most noiseless and dreamlike manner, amidst the cheers of the people who lined the sides of the canal, and passed under the beautifully decorated bridges belonging to the villages connected with the last coalpits belonging to Lord Ellesmere. In half an hour we were at the landing place in Worsley Park, and in five minutes at the hall door . . . The evening was so wet and thick that one could not see beyond the windows."

The Old Duke referred to in the Queen's diary is none other than the Iron Duke of Wellington, victor of Waterloo and much beloved mentor of Victoria, having been Prime Minister in the early years following her coronation. Captain Egerton was the second son of Lord Egerton who, by this time, was lame with gout and walked only with the aid of a stick. The weather seems to have been typical of many a Test Match Saturday at Old Trafford but the Queen does seem to have enjoyed her journey on the Royal barge. Following Victoria's visit this was used as the Ellesmere's private vessel and was only broken up at Stretford in 1948. In view of the recent development of the canal systems as tourist attractions, it is a pity that this happened. It would have made a splendid focus for a boat museum which we feel should have been established at Worsley.

The Bridgewater had another memorable Royal occasion in 1869 when the Prince of Wales travelled from Worsley and along the canal to a regatta on the Irwell. Oarsmen from Salford pitted their strength and skill against those from Manchester, the two settlements being separated by the river. Apparently, one rowing crew, whilst standing upright in their delicately balanced craft, had the boat sink beneath them as they raised their oars on high to salute the Prince.

These and other recorded events would seem to suggest that, initially at least, the canal withstood the economic threat posed by the railway. There was, however, no way that progress of the railway could be kept at bay for ever as the Duke of Bridgewater had predicted on the very day his canal was first opened to traffic.

Bridgewater House at Runcorn. A delightful Georgian house used by the Duke as he supervised the construction of the Mersey link to the Bridgewater Canal. The house still stands to the left of the Ship Canal, but the Bridgewater basin further to the left has been filled in.

The Trustees seemed always to be hard pressed for cash to compete with the railways, but they also had to finance the essential improvements needed to keep their coal mines open and producing the type of fuel demanded by new industries. The construction of coke ovens, for example, were a constant drain on capital. Pressure mounted throughout the 1860s to sell the canal to railway companies, although in hindsight we can see that some individuals had shares in both canals and railways and had therefore a vested interest in take-overs which allowed them to reap rich dividends.

In 1872, these pressures led to the setting up of the Bridgewater Navigation Company Limited and its first business enterprise was to raise the enormous sum of £1,120,000 to pursuade the Trustees to relinquish control of the canal. This did not go down at all well in Worsley. Then, as now, people believed that amalgamations always resulted in redundancies. It is also easy to see why many legal executives grew rich from working out how to circumvent the Old Duke's will.

Further economic pressure was soon to follow as the Manchester Ship Canal was proposed, and being unashamedly aimed at creating an inland seaport of world, as opposed to only national, importance. The main opposition to its construction was obviously going to come from the rich merchants of Liverpool but the Manchester Ship Canal Company had equally powerful industrialists supporting the enterprise.

The presence of a larger and more modern canal so close to the Bridgewater was bound to take away a high percentage of its revenue. It was also obvious to both canal companies that during the construction of the Ship Canal there would be considerable disruption to movement along the Bridgewater, with some actual physical reconstructions and perhaps realignments being required. These included the replacement of the Barton aqueduct. The only logical solution was a merger, or rather an all out take over bid for the old canal.

A bid of £1,710,000 was finally accepted for the Bridgewater Canal and all its assets. This represented a·profit of more than half a million pounds for the directors of the Bridgewater Navigation Company. Its short life between 1872 and 1885 had been very profitable indeed — equal at least to the wildest dreams of the most ambitious businessmen.

The Manchester Ship Canal Company then operated their two waterways in partnership and, initially, maintained impressive levels of profitability despite the development of the railway network. The Company also continued to run the Bridgewater Collieries until just after the First World War when they sold them to the Manchester Collieries which themselves were nationalised in 1948.

The sale of the mines brought to an end the link between coal and water which stimulated the construction of the Duke's canal in the first place. At the same time the Egerton estates, including their extensive lands in and around Worsley, came up for sale. The requirements of the Old Duke's will had by then lapsed, but during the build up to and the period of the First World War, all of the business brains were concentrated upon the fight for Europe. In 1923 the Bridgewater Estate Limited took over the Old Duke's enterprise and continued to oversee the lands until 1984 when Peel Holdings plc purchased them.

The link between the canal and the old Bridgewater Estate was, however, soon to be reforged. In 1987 Highams Limited took control of the Ship Canal but then amalgamated with Peel Holdings plc. The Bridgewater Canal is now once more beneath the same financial umbrella as the Manchester Ship Canal and is managed by their Property Division. This division has been of great assistance during the preparation of this manuscript.

As we have seen, there is now a working association between the Ship Canal Company and the Bridgewater Canal Trust, a union which has existed since the Bollin aqueduct leakage of 1971. Although the Bridgewater Canal continued to operate as an industrial waterway until 1974, its place has been taken by the leisure industry which is now expanding. This is likely to continue into the next century.

The Bridgewater is a vital link in what has become known as the Cheshire Ring, which allows leisure craft to pass easily from the Southern and Midland Canal network to those in the north, such as the Rochdale which is also steadily being restored. This is now open along most of its length and the Leeds to Liverpool has remained a highly functional trans-Pennine link. Although the Runcorn link into the Mersey is now closed, the Leeds to Liverpool terminus at Stanley Dock is still open.

We can remember in the early 1950s when a few intrepid souls flew in the face of convention and launched pleasure craft onto the canals. In 1971 almost 600 private barges and cruisers chugged their happy way along the Bridgewater. In the mid 1970s a friend of ours kept a diary in which he recorded the changes that he observed along the canal and he also kept a list of the wildlife seen during his cruises. His records included breeding kingfishers, herons feeding alongside the cut, cormorants and goosanders successfully fishing in the canal, mute swans resident along most of its length and he also noted an impressive assortment of aquatic flowers such as water mint, crowfoot, yellow flag, ragged robin, butterbur, coltsfoot and lady's smock. On one occasion we watched a family of red breasted merganser with the young following the female and looking like a line of men of war in full sail.

All these natural delights make cruising any canal a joy and, in recent years, it has been interesting to note the gradual spread of wildlife from the rural areas into the heart of the industrial towns and cities. Doubtless this spread is due to the decline in the traditional industries but it cannot be denied that practical conservation measures have also had a beneficial effect.

The Canal Company take great pains to control the traffic along the cut granting in the order of 1000 moorings each year. These are divided between cruising clubs with private members and commercially operated vessels, all of which are provided with facilities which compare favourably with those offered on other Inland Waterways.

The 1990s have emphasised the increase in the use of water as a recreational resource and as this is likely to continue, the future for the Bridgewater Canal looks brighter than has been the case for more than a century since the Manchester Ship Canal was opened.

The Ellesmere Port Boat Museum

ELLESMERE PORT BOAT MUSEUM is reached via the M56 and M53 motorways and leaving at junction 9. The museum is open throughout the year, there is a shop, information centre and parties, including school and other groups are welcome. There is good access for disabled visitors and a well appointed conference centre is being used more and more by businesses. There is a library and archive centre which can be used by anyone interested in the history of canals in Britain.

At the end of the 18th century the area now known as Ellesmere Port was little more than a small collection of fishermens' cottages called Netherpool overlooking the Mersey. To inland based industrialists the Mersey gave access to the sea, and Shropshire potteries envisaged a canal linking the Severn and the Dee to the Mersey. By 1795 the link was complete, with work done by William Jessop as engineer and with Thomas Telford as the architect. By the 1840s the new basin was linked to a number of canals but also incorporating some railways. The canals became known as the Shropshire Union, or more affectionately as the "Shroppie". Much of the finance came from the town of Ellesmere, and the new complex and the outlet to the sea became known as Ellesmere Port.

The Boat Museum is based around an early broad lock and a later narrow lock, the latter using less water to operate, but both of which linked into a basin where ocean going ships could exchange cargo with the canal barges and narrow boats. The warehouses around the basin have been converted into private housing. There are a number of interesting vessels in the basin including the tug Daniel Adamson. This was named after one of the men who founded the Manchester Ship Canal and after its service as a tug the vessel was used as an Inspection vessel.

Above the basin is an old canal warehouse which was built in 1871 to store wheat for the Kelloggs factories. Here are more interesting boats including the Mossdale, a Mersey flat built in the 1870s. These flats where sea going but could also penetrate the broad canals including part of the Shropshire Union and the stretch of the Leeds to Liverpool Canal as far as Wigan. This meant that there were several points where links were possible into the Bridgewater.

Canal maintenance was not easy or cheap and

two of the biggest problems were weeds in summer and ice in winter. Special boats were needed to deal with these and on display are a weed cutting barge dating to around 1930 and an ice breaker of the late 19th century. The latter had specially strengthened sides and which was rocked from side to side by a strong crew, who must have been physically and mentally tough to work in such conditions. Close to the ice breaker is a steam powered tunnel tug built about 1912. These tugs were kept at such places as Foulridge on the Leeds to Liverpool Canal and used to pull barges through long tunnels whilst the horses were taken along the surface to meet the barges at the other end. The tunnel tugs saved men known as leggers the cold back breaking job of lying on planks at the edge of the barge and pushing against the walls of the tunnel with their feet.

The principle was that those who used the waterways paid and tolls were levied. At Ellesmere Boat Museum a splendid early 19th century toll house and office has been converted into a museum in which are displayed the merchandise carried along the canal. In the 1930s a lady inspector, who was a qualified nurse, was based here to ensure that the bargees' children were kept healthy and educated.

We had great fun watching modern day schoolchildren enjoying the freedom of being allowed to handle candle tallow, cotton, coal, soap, salt and of course pottery which was the main reason for the construction of the Shropshire Union Canal.

The Wedgwood family of potters, who were acquainted with the Duke of Bridgewater, put a lot of money into canals and it is easy to understand why when you consider what rough roads could do to delicate china.

Each day vessels pass through the locking system of the museum, which is kept in full working order, and on most days boat trips are on offer. It is great fun to have the feeling of being carried up and down a lock and listening to the mighty rush of water.

There are so many outdoor and indoor exhibits at the Boat Museum that it needs several visits to see all its treasures and is value for money whatever the weather. Look out in particular for the blacksmith working in the old stables. The barge horses may have gone, but the sound of iron on anvil and the sight of flying sparks is always exciting.

No student of the Bridgewater Canal should miss the Boat Museum even though the two are only indirectly connected. There is no museum specifically related to the Bridgewater but the Boat Museum has boats, large numbers of photographs and other archive material which relate to the Duke's Cut.

We would suggest not one visit to this museum but two. Go first, then explore the Bridgewater, and return a second time. You will be surprised how much you have missed. The staff here are so enthusiastic that they will persuade us to take another canal journey — perhaps along the Shroppie Union which has just as many tales to tell as our own beloved Bridgewater.

Along the canal towards the village of Moore.

Above: Dunham Massey Georgian orangary.

Left: Dunham Massey fallow deer.

Opposite page: Dunham Massey moat.

The end of the present line of the Bridgewater Canal at Runcorn. Waterloo Bridge is now swamped by a modern road system.